The Army correspondence of Colonel John Laurens in The years 1777-8

John Laurens, Henry Laurens

W.M. Gilmore Simms

Alpha Editions

This edition published in 2019

ISBN : 9789353708368

Design and Setting By
Alpha Editions
email - alphaedis@gmail.com

Bradford Club Series.

NUMBER SEVEN.

John Laurens.

THE
ARMY CORRESPONDENCE
OF
COLONEL JOHN LAURENS
IN THE YEARS 1777-8

NOW FIRST PRINTED FROM ORIGINAL LETTERS ADDRESSED
TO HIS FATHER

HENRY LAURENS

𝔓𝔯𝔢𝔰𝔦𝔡𝔢𝔫𝔱 𝔬𝔣 ℭ𝔬𝔫𝔤𝔯𝔢𝔰𝔰

WITH A MEMOIR

BY

WM. GILMORE SIMMS

NEW YORK
M DCCC LXVII

SUBSCRIBER'S COPY.

No.

SEVENTY-FIVE COPIES PRINTED.

PUBLICATIONS

OF THE

BRADFORD CLUB.

THE BRADFORD CLUB.

UNDER this designation, a few gentlemen, interested in the study of American History and Literature, propose occasionally to print limited editions of such manuscripts and scarce pamphlets as may be deemed of value towards illustrating these subjects. They will seek to obtain for this purpose unpublished journals or correspondence containing matter worthy of record, and which may not properly be included in the Historical Collections or Documentary Histories of the several States. Such unpretending contemporary chronicles often throw precious light upon the motives of action and the imperfectly narrated events of bygone days; perhaps briefly touched upon in dry official documents.

The Club may also issue fac-similes of curious manuscripts or documents worthy of notice, which, like the printed issues, will bear its imprint.

> "These are the
> Registers, the chronicles of the age
> They were written in, and speak the truth of History
> Better than a hundred of your printed
> Communications."— *Shakerly Marmyon's Antiquary.*

WILLIAM BRADFORD — the first New York Printer — whose name the Club has adopted, came to this country in 1682, and established his Press in the neighborhood of Philadelphia. In 1693 he removed to this City — was appointed Royal Printer — and set up his Press "at the Sign of the Bible" For upwards of thirty years he was the only Printer in the Province, and in 1725 published our first Newspaper — *The New York Gazette.* He conducted this paper until 1743 when he retired from business. He died in May, 1752, and was described, in an obituary notice of the day, as " a man of great sobriety and industry, a real friend to the poor and needy, and kind and affable to all." He was buried in Trinity Church Yard, by the side of the wife of his youth ; and the loving affection of relatives and friends reared a simple and unostentatious Monument to his memory.

MEMOIR OF JOHN LAURENS.

The collection of original letters which follow in this volume, written during the war of the American revolution and at the most interesting of its several crises, and now for the first time published, will, we are assured, prove not only agreeable to the general reader, but a most valuable contribution to the material of American history. They are from the pen of John Laurens, a native of South Carolina, a lieutenant colonel in the American army, a favorite aid de camp of General Washington, frequently acting as his private secretary, and highly valued by that great man, in every capacity, as one in whose honor, valor and judgment he could equally confide.

John Laurens was a son of Henry Laurens for some time president of the Continental congress, subsequently a minister plenipotentiary to Holland, and finally, under commission of congress one of the ministers with Franklin and Jay in the negotiation of the treaty of peace between Great Britain and the United States.

John Laurens was born somewhere about 1756, and was a student of law in London at the opening of the revolution. His letters to his father, uncle, and others of his family, begin prior to this period, and are deeply imbued with the politics of the times as currently expressed in Great Britain. Several of these have been preserved, though they do not appear in this collection. They are all characterized by good taste, a style at once easy, natural and impressive, a nice observance of the proprieties, quite remarkable in one so young, showing a well trained and well balanced mind, with sentiment, thoughtful opinion, fine sensibilities and the most ardent patriotism. They exhibit also a constant endeavor at solid acquisition, and the search for it, usually, in the most proper and profitable directions.

From the letters not included in this collection, which, for unity, are confined exclusively to the army correspondence, we learn that he was at Westminster, pursuing his studies, in April, 1772. He was then sixteen years of age. His hand writing, even at this time, which subsequently became admirably perfected, for symmetry, grace and uniformity, was remarkably indicative of character and force, coupled with compactness and great clearness, showing the attributes of a strong mind and will, already under self-restraint.

Soon after this date he visited the continent, and in August of the same year, he writes from Geneva,

whither he has gone for his studies in some of the
higher branches of education. In 1773, he reports
the progress he has made in the study of the civil
law and mathematics, under some of the great masters
of Geneva, then one of the most famous schools of
letters and philosophy upon the continent. He has
completed his course in ancient and modern history,
as it was then pursued, and has begun his readings
and reviews in political eloquence, which, at that
period, was a necessary part in the education of a
gentleman even where he contemplated no practice in
the profession. But Geneva was held to be a dangerous province in which to frame the mind, if not the
morals of the youthful student, and young Laurens,
writing to his parents, is at pains to show them that
he is able to mantain his faith, in spite of the influence of great names, and the authoritative opinions of
society. He has asserted the independence of his
own mind, and, while receiving information and acquir-
ing knowledge, he has fallen into none of the fashions
of infidelity. Even then, though but seventeen, he was
not to be overawed, into self-abnegation, by any mere
name, however potent as a social authority. He avows
his utter disregard of, if not disrespect, for what was
skeptical in the teachings of the doctors of Geneva, of
whose influence his father might well entertain many
fears in the case of a son, at once so bold, earnest, and
enthusiastic. But he had no cause for anxiety. The
letters of the son disabuse him of his fears — if he ever

really entertained them — in terms of great good sense and modest firmness. In pursuing this topic, the writer is enabled to give an interesting account of the state of religion and of church practice and discipline at Geneva, during his continuance in that place.

It is about this period, and while at Geneva, that his letters begin to display a certain degree of doubt and anxiety, in respect to his choice of a profession. This is a problem of great embarrassment to every really conscientious student; since it implies the first necessary inquiry: "What am I best fitted for? What can I best do?" — the choice depending, in the case of the honest mind, solely upon the endowment. Young Laurens felt all the embarrassments of this problem, the tastes and impulses naturally tending to that interference with the judgment, which constitutes the great difficulty in the way of deciding justly upon the right of the individual to choose from the professions, or, indeed, to attempt the professions at all — the qualities which justify (with proper training and education) the entrance upon a professional career, being special gifts to the individual, and not the common allotment of a race or people.

Laurens treats his subject with all the ingenuousness of boyhood, though without hitting the exact rule which we have indicated, and which requires that the choice of the profession must be governed wholly by a just regard to the endowments of the individual. A neglect of this rule is probably one of the most mischievous of all the educational influences of society, as it so constantly elevates incompetence to office and authority.

Two of the letters of young Laurens, which now lie before us, addressed to his uncle, fully illustrate the frank and ingenuous nature of the youth, the seriousness of his purpose even in boyhood, the elevation and ardency of his aim, and the high toned honor and purity of those motives and principles which marked his career through life. Nor will the simplicity with which he declares these motives, fail to arrest attention as significant of an ingenuousness of nature which denied no concealments. In one of these letters, of date April 17, 1772, he says: "For my own part I find it exceedingly difficult, even at this time, to determine in which of the learned professions I shall list myself. When I hear a man of an improved education, speak from the goodness of heart divine truths with a persuasive eloquence which commands the most solemn silence and serious attention from all his audience, my soul burns to be in his place; when I hear of one who shines at the bar, and overpowers chicanery and oppression, who pleads the cause of helpless widows and injured orphans, who, at the same time that he gains lasting fame to himself, dispenses benefits to multitudes, the same emulous ardor rises in my heart. When I hear of another who has done eminent service to mankind, by discovering remedies for the numerous train of disorders to which our frail bodies are continually subject, and has given relief to numbers whose lives, without his assistance, would have been insupportable burdens, I cannot refrain from wishing to be an equal dispenser of good.

"Thus am I agitated. 'Tis beyond, far beyond the power of one man to shine conspicuous in all these characters: one must be determined upon: and I am almost persuaded that it would be that of the divine, if this did not preclude me from bearing arms in defence of my country — for I cannot read with indifference the valiant acts of those, whose prudent conduct and admirable bravery have rescued the liberties of their countrymen, and deprived their enemies of power to do them hurt.

"No particular profession is in itself disagreeable to me. Each promises some share of fame. I never loved merchandise, nor can I now. There are but three considerations that can reconcile it to me, first, that the universal correspondence which it establishes, gives one a knowledge of mankind: then the continual flow of money peculiar to this employment, enables a man to do extensive good to individuals of distressed fortunes, without injuring himself, as well as to promote works of public utility, upon the most beneficial terms.

"Many such instances have offered to my attention, but I am sure the recital of one will give you pleasure. A man from Scotland trumped up a claim against our landlord, Mr. Deans, pretended for maintenance of a former wife; swore to a debt, and sued him for £300 and upwards, and carried him away to a bailiff's sponging house; but papa relieved him the same day. The man, finding that Deans had a liberal and hearty friend, made some application to papa, who told him generally, but positively, that if Mr. Deans was on the right side, he should not want a thousand guineas to do him justice; if on the other hand he was in the wrong he should not receive the assistance of a half-penny from *him;* then left the man abruptly. This wrought such an effect, that the man offered to submit the whole matter to papa; but he would not engage in it. Then the bold claimant offered to drop the action entirely if Mr. Deans would pay half the charges. Papa said he would soon be glad to go off without any other benefit, than that of escaping the pillory. If Deans had not been supported by such a friend, he would have remained in gaol, under scandalous imputations, and probably have been totally ruined, for he had tried all his London acquaintance in vain. The man, at length, begged of Mr. Deans to accept a general release: which he in his good nature did; he signed a release, discharged Deans's bail, and went immediately out of England; but papa says, if *he* had been previously consulted, he would have turned the tables upon him for example's sake."

It is a boy's letter; but the letter of a very remarkable boy. The second, dated more than two years later (Sept. 15, 1774) from the same place, exhibits the matured resolve of his mind on the subject of his previous embarrassment. He has made his choice, giving to the law his preference among the professions. "My present prospect," he writes, "is either to be lodged in the Temple or in some reputable private family, under the eye of an honest lawyer, if such a one can be found, and to study the laws of my country very diligently for three years. But a horrible prospect it is, that I am to get my bread by the quarrels and disputes of others, so that I can't pray for success in my occupation without praying at the same time that a great part of mankind may be in error either through ignorance or design. The only noble part of my profession is utterly unprofitable in this world, I mean the defence of the weak and oppressed; it is a part, however, that I am determined never to neglect; for, although it enriches not, it must make a man happy. What can be equal to the heartfelt satisfaction which abounds in him who pleads the cause of the fatherless and the widow, and sees right done to him that suffers wrong. Thus, after long wavering, I am now fixed: no more talk to me either of physic or commerce; law is the knotty subject which I must endeavor to render pleasant."

In Nov., 1774, he reports further progress in this direction. In a letter from Chancery lane, he says:

"On Monday I shall be initiated in the mystery of mutton-eating, by which, alone, I can gain the title of barrister. I have entered into the necessary bond, and paid the accustomed fees to the present time."

His letters, during the period over which we have gone, show him to have been an active observer of affairs and a weigher of opinion in Great Britain, and are full of references to the antagonist relations, growing daily more and more embittered, between that nation and its American colonies. His mind seems to have been equally well informed in English opinion and American principles. The politics of both sections are discussed, or at least considered, and passages from them, even now, would be found to possess an interest for the American reader; but these must be reserved for other publications. We give a single sample from a letter addressed to his uncle, of date 13th Nov., 1775. It is partly of this character: and shows, besides, the impatient workings of his own spirit, encaged as it were, chafing at the restraint of his abode in England, while his father and his country are preparing, in anxious apprehensions, for the terrors of the impending war.

"Can I think with composure of HIS [his father] being continually exposed to danger, while I am remote in security. Although he commands me absolutely to obey him, is not what may be my duty in one sense, baseness and want of true affection in another? O God! I know not what to do! — of what avail are wishes? When is the time for an active part, if not the present. No one can conceive what I feel for my dearest friend and father; to ransom him, I would give my life with pleasure: I do not

3

mean to boast, for I think it little to give; but it is
my all.

" I endeavored to gain admission into the House of
Commons to-day, but in vain: Mr. Burke had been
speaking to ———, when I was dancing a fruitless
attendance at the door. But to what end these elo-
quent harangues, if ministry outvote; and our fine
speeches are [only] printed; in the beginning of the
session there seemed to be some hope of accommodation, but now I think 'tis vanished.

" Duchess of Bedford, it is said, has some pique
against her brother, Lord Gower, and, to give him
trouble, will bring over to the minority her dependents.
But the ministry are so powerful that a large defec-
tion from their party will not be missed. Since Lord
Geo. Germaine, and Lord Weymouth have succeeded
to office the prospect of affairs has blackened."

In another style and mood, we give an extract from
a letter preceding this in time, addressed to his sister.
It exhibits the affectionate tenderness of his character
in its domestic relations: the delicacy of its tone and
tenor, as well as the considerate prudence of the
writer, illustrating the claim which is made on his
behalf, as that of the graceful and courteous gentleman. He is still, it must be remembered, but a youth,
having barely reached his nineteenth year. The letter
is dated 5th May, 1775.

" Write instantly, clearly, fully ; and explain to me,
my sweet sister, that little sentence dictated by a

tender heart, and which seems to have cost you a sigh
in writing it. What is that important something
which agitates your mind, and demands the friendly
aid of a confidant? Make one of your brother, or our
indulgent father; you cannot doubt of *our* love.
Whatever it be, depend upon the best advice I am
capable of; but let me entreat you, my dear, to banish
reserve, and write to me as freely as you would indulge
your own ideas in tranquil retirement. The conference which you so ardently wish for, cannot happen
soon: in unbosoming one's self, there are some
advantages in writing, if we may believe Mr. Pope:—

> The virgin's wish, without her fears impart,
> Excuse the blush, and pour out all the heart:—

though I can very well conceive of circumstances
which require more of detail and minute explanation,
than a letter easily admits of. But you write to a
friend; the form of the letter is not essential; the
length will not be complained of. 'Tis true, that in
a conversation, your confidence would be regulated
in a great measure by the encouragement given you;
but consider me as your other self: approving, or
ready in finding excuses, and write as you would
speak upon such an occasion. I shall make many
fruitless conjectures. As your letter contains symp-
toms of something grave, I must needs be in painful
suspense till you put it in my power to assist you.

No more need be said to procure me a satisfactory letter upon this subject."

The residence of John Laurens in Europe, during the intervals between the years 1772 and 1775, was occupied by other griefs, anxieties and interests than those of study and politics. By a cruel accident, during his temporary absence from London, a younger brother, a most promising boy, and a great favorite with his father, whom the latter had left in Europe also, with the view to his education, was killed by an accidental fall while at play. The sensitive nature of John Laurens prompted him to bitter self reproaches, on this occasion, for which there was no good reason. The boy had been, indeed, entrusted measurably to his care and keeping; but he does not seem to have neglected any proper precautions in his case; and the casualty is to be ascribed wholly to the indiscreet playfulness of the boy, in a caprice of sport, such as is common to, and characteristic of childhood. But the keenness of the pang and the terrible suddenness of the event, seem for the moment, to have overcome his judgment; his sensibilities were too active for his thoughts, and he made a case of conscience out of the event, which embittered the natural sorrow, and humbled greatly the spirit beyond the usual exactions of grief.

We have reason to believe, from the results in the development of intellect and character, that he pursued his studies with diligence and zeal. But his nature was warm, and craved sympathy; and to this we are to ascribe his premature, and, in a worldly sense, perhaps, imprudent marriage, which took place only a short period before his departure for America. But, even while taking his vows at the altar, they were made with the accompanying avowal of his resolution to proceed to his native country, in spite of all other obligations, and join himself in arms with his people. Opportunity for this, however, was not easy, and he watched the occasion with the avidity of a patriotic zeal, which soon realized its object. The opportunity at length presented itself; the contingency for which he had awaited finally came, and tearing himself away from his young bride, he made his way from England into France, the only route by which he could then find his way to America. His first letter (which we quote) to his uncle, James Laurens, dates from Paris, 11th January, 1777.

" My Dear Uncle :

I arrived here the 7th inst., and have since had the pleasure of conversing, at three different times, with Doctor Franklin. His accounts of America are, that she will be much better provided for, the ensuing campaign, than she was for the last; that the members of the congress are as unanimous, as the members of popular assemblies generally are; and that the spirit of the people does not, by any means, flag. It is a secret yet whether France will assist America or not.

The fact, as it appears to me, is, that France does not choose to involve herself in a war by declaring herself openly, when she can give special succors without any risk. There are more French officers in America than can find employment; the French ports are daily receiving American vessels. Some time ago, two armed vessels, one of which was loaded with military stores, were cleared out for St. Domingo, and a number of French officers took their passages in them. By some means or other, Lord Stormont discovered that these vessels were employed by Silas Deane, and the cargoes intended for America. He went immediately, at an unusual hour for business, to Versailles, and represented the matter to M. de Vergennes, minister and secretary for the foreign department; he had obtained an exact list of every thing on board; said he had sufficient proof that the whole was designed for the rebellious English colonies; and demanded that these vessels should be stopped. The answer was that a courier should be dispatched; a courier was dispatched, but the bird had flown.

"To-night, I take place in the diligence for Bordeaux, from whence I hope soon to embark for my own country. Cochran has sailed, which I am very sorry for, as my acquaintance with him, and the good character of his vessel, made me wish to be his passenger.

"Present my tenderest love to my dear aunt and sisters. I am afraid I shall not be able to write to

my dear Patty. That God may grant you all his
blessing, is the constant prayer of your most affectionate

JOHN LAURENS."

The defeat of the British fleet, under Sir Peter
Parker, in Charleston harbor, was, in all probability,
the event which more immediately prompted this
resolution to fling aside his studies, professions and
other ties. This event, which happened on the 28th
June, 1776, was not known in England until the 22d
August, of the same year.

According to the purpose expressed in the preceding letter, Laurens made his way to America, *via* Cape
François, which place he reached somewhere about
the 3d April, 1777. In thirteen days thereafter, we
find him safely arrived in South Carolina, where he at
once joined the American army. He was soon after
transferred to the main force of the Continentals, at
the north, there being no longer any enemy threaten-
ing the safety of the south.

He was now under the immediate command and
eye of Washington. The relations which had long
existed between the commander-in-chief and Henry
Laurens, then president of congress, were of the most
grateful and confidential character. These naturally
secured for young Laurens the *entrée*, under the most
favorable auspices, into the family of Washington.
His own qualities did the rest. The grace, spirit,

accomplishments, excellent sense and general intelligence of the young soldier, combined to confirm him in position on his own account, and, like Hamilton, he soon became the trusted agent of his chief, his secretary as well as aid and confidant.

But these relations did not keep him from the field of action, which was the province he most preferred. He sought every opportunity for active service, and distinguished himself, on all occasions, especially at the battle of Germantown, where he was wounded in the endeavor to expel the enemy from Chew's house, where they had established themselves in a hold too strong to be wrested from them by the inadequate means provided for the occasion. He was engaged in the brilliant though capricious and indecisive conflicts on the plains of Monmouth, where the base conduct, if not treachery, of Charles Lee, came nigh to bring about the most disastrous consequences. On this occasion he acquired large increase of reputation for brilliant dash and determined courage. In Rhode Island he added anew to his reputation both as a sage counsellor and as a military man. In reference to his bravery in his campaign in the latter state Washington wrote to his father Henry Laurens:—"Feeling myself interested in every occurrence that tends to the honor of your worthy son; and sensible of the pleasure it must give you to hear his just plaudit, I take the liberty of transcribing a paragraph of General Greene's letter to me giving some account of the

conduct of particular officers in the action on Rhode
Island. Our troops behaved with great spirit, and
the brigade of militia under the command of General Lovel advanced with great resolution and in good
order; and stood the fire of the enemy with great
firmness. Lt. Col. Livingston, Col. Jackson and Col.
H. B. Livingston did themselves great honor in the
transactions of the day. But it is not in my power to
do justice to Col. Laurens who acted both the general
and partisan. His command of regular troops was
small, but he did every thing possible to be done by
their numbers." [1]

He was about to change the scene of operations.
The war languished at the north. The British had
begun their demonstrations in force against Georgia
and North Carolina, and Laurens eagerly sought and
obtained leave to repair to the defence of his native
state. He joined the militia forces under Moultrie,
led the troops which defended the passes of the
Coosohatchie, was wounded and narrowly escaped
with his life and from captivity. His horse was killed
under him, and but for the devotion of a few friends
and adherents, he must have perished or been made
a prisoner. Subsequently, he was one of the favorite
lieutenants of Moultrie in the attempted *coup de main*
of Prevost against Charleston.

---

[1] Manuscript letter of Washington to Henry Laurens; Whiteplains,
Sept. 4, 1778.

4

Savannah had already fallen into the hands of the British; and Lincoln, then in command of the army of the south, upon the arrival of the French fleet, under Count D'Estaing, proceeded to attempt the recovery of the capital of Georgia. Savannah was strongly fortified by the British, who took advantage of an indiscreet indulgence in point of time, accorded them by D'Estaing, prior to the arrival of Lincoln. When the allies advanced to the assault upon the place, to Col. Laurens was confided the command of the American light infantry. At the head of his command, he led them on to the attack with his accustomed dash and headlong gallantry, and was one of the first to mount the British redoubts. We know from general history the issue of this badly managed leaguer and assault. The combined forces of America and France met with a decided defeat, and all farther attempts to secure the city from the grasp of the enemy were abandoned as hopeless. The French retired to their shipping and left the country, while the Americans under Lincoln retreated across the Savannah river into South Carolina.

It followed as a matter of course from the failure of this enterprise, that South Carolina should suffer next from British invasion. Lincoln with his small force of five thousand men including the local militia, threw himself unwisely into Charleston, where he was soon besieged by the British under Sir Henry Clinton, with a well provided army of twelve thousand. The cooperation of a powerful fleet enabled him to close up all the avenues to the city by sea and land, and after a gallant defence of nearly two months and the exhaustion of the provisions of the garrison, the American General was compelled to capitulate.

During the siege, Laurens was conspicuous as usual as well in the council as the field. He led at the head of his light troops, in the few sorties that were made, displaying on all occasions that headlong enthusiastic gallantry, which was sometimes condemned as temerity, but which had the good effect usually of inspiring confidence in his troops, encouraging those who faltered, and lessening those ideas of British superiority and resource which were quite too general in America at this period, and which were particularly calculated to impair the resolution of a provincial militia. He was one of those leaders who never know when they are beaten — a characteristic which in war is very much like a virtue, and which is decidedly to be preferred to that soldiership which never knows in season when it is victorious!

After the fall of Charleston, Laurens again resumed his relations with the grand army under Washington. But that army presented at this time nothing encouraging in its aspects. It had dwindled away in numbers and the states were slow to recruit it. The country was impoverished, if not exhausted. Continued progress and repeated successes on the part of

the invader, with the rapid diminution of the national
resources of the country under a long protracted
external pressure, had brought the congress and the
people at large to a sense of weariness. The crisis,
more perilous than ever before, had made doubtful their
hopes of independence. It was now evident, as an
essential condition of success, that without further
foreign aid, especially in money, there could not much
longer be continued any adequate resistance to the
external pressure. It was resolved accordingly that
fresh appeals should be made to France for a far larger
degree of assistance than she had ever before accorded
to the wants of the colonies. For this mission, a special messenger was required directly from the army,
having equally the confidence of Washington and
Congress and bearing the letters of the former along
with the commission of the latter.

It was undoubtedly the highest sort of compliment
but not, as we shall see, an unmerited one, that both of
these parties should unite upon the youthful aid de
camp of the commander in chief. The choice origin-
ally was that of Washington himself, and it was
promptly concurred in by the congress. At this period
Laurens was but twenty-five years old. We have but
few instances on record — none that we can recall —
of the choice, by any nation, of one so young as an
envoy extraordinary. One of the youngest of all the
officers by whom Washington was surrounded, he was
required to execute a mission of the most vital im-

portance and of the greatest delicacy. But in a well
known phrase, Laurens carried an old head upon young
shoulders. He was a man of thought as well as
action; who could design as well as execute, and was
possessed of peculiar personal advantages. Himself of
French origin, of the well known and much honored
Huguenot stock, he was a master of the French
language, and did not need the intervention of an
interpreter. He was well read in civil law; had studied politics, or rather statesmanship, as something of
a science, and was quite familiar with the old and new
world histories. Practiced in the graces, of noble form
and figure, he had the facility and manners if not the
arts of the courtier; and with all these virtues of
grace, manner, education and acquisition, he possessed that sort of boldness and energy which belongs
to great ardency of temperament and a resolute will,
qualities which in some degree at that time, but more
particularly since, distinguish the American character,
and render its frankness more than a match for the
subtleties of the mere politician, or the native refine-
ments of the ordinary courtier. In all respects, he
was far more variously endowed for such a mission
than the greater number of his countrymen of even
twice his age. It is also to be remembered that he
had been for a long time intimately associated, on an
equal footing and in like relations to Washington, with
one of the ablest of American statesmen in the person
of Alexander Hamilton. Briefly, his capacity for the

mission was such as fully to justify the choice of the commander in chief, even if the results of his labor had failed to do so.

Laurens reached Paris in February, 1781, and promptly sought an interview with Franklin, then the resident minister, who gave him no encouragement in regard to the prospects of his mission. He had himself failed of that degree of success which was essential to the needs of his country, and which would have made the succor of France efficacious for the American cause in the struggle with her powerful adversary. The great philosopher, it was thought by many, had yielded to the seduction of a brilliant but frivolous court, and had shown himself less earnest in the advocacy of the claims of his country, in urging her necessities than was consistent with a fervid patriotism.[1] It is thought that he somewhat resented the employment of another, and one so young, for the attainment of those very objects which were specially involved in his own commission,—and this was natural enough. He was, in fact, temporarily, though not formally superseded. At all events, he gave no assistance to the new commissioner, beyond bringing him to the knowledge of the minister Vergennes. To him Laurens addressed himself with all the earnestness of his nature, stimulated to fervency by a perfect know-

[1] See Memoirs of Arthur Lee.

ledge of the condition of the American army and
the rapidly failing resources of the country. His
quest was generally for succor in arms and the
munitions of war, but especially to negotiate for
a large loan of money. It was in financial respects
that the American people were reduced to extremity.

But his labours to persuade and convince Vergennes
were all in vain. That minister would not or could
not see the extent of American exigency. He was
cold, indifferent and evasive. His self-complacency
would not allow him to be hurried, and by a mere
youth, who might well be supposed an inexpert; while
the formalities as well as the frivolities of a court and
its etiquette, were of themselves great obstacles in the
path of a singled-eyed and ardent patriotism. But the
mission of Laurens would not brook delay. For two
months Vergennes had contrived to baffle the direct
approaches of the youthful commissioner. But he
little knew the spirit, temper and resources of the
young man. Laurens was resolved to be baffled no
longer, and he proceeded to cut the knot that he was
not suffered to untie. He determined, in defiance of
all form and precedent, to make his appeal directly
from the minister to the monarch! This purpose he
declared to Franklin, who discouraged the proceeding,
as against all rule and etiquette, and refused, in any
way, to give his countenance to the attempt. Vergennes, also, to whom he avowed his purpose, was
confounded at his audacity, and probably deceived

himself with the belief that the threat was simply
designed for himself, and to expedite his own
movements, and that, after his own declared hos-
tility to such a course of action, he should hear no
more of it.

He was mistaken. He little knew his man. Laurens cherished his purpose faithfully, and it was a
surprise to Vergennes himself, when at the first public
levee which followed, he carried his purpose into
action. It was then first, after so long a delay, that
he received audience of the king. The reception was
general and simply formal, and not designed with
any view to business. The monarch, according to
custom, received the parties, ambassadors and distinguished persons from abroad, accorded them a
simple recognition, and they passed on severally,
without a moment's delay, giving place to others.
The court was one of severe etiquette, and a rigid
formality which was confounded with ideas of state
and dignity. It was, therefore, with something like a
sentiment of terror, that the court beheld the young
ambassador, instead of simply bowing and passing
forward like the rest, come to a full stop in the presence of his majesty, and present his memorial: while
in good set terms, in French, in well chosen words,
few but forcible, he made known his business, and
the exigencies of the American cause. He took
occasion, in the few brief moments in which he thus
trespassed upon etiquette, to report to the king, that

he was recently from America, from the camp of Washington; that he bore the mission of that great man, as well as that of congress; that he personally knew the truth of all the facts which he reported, and concluded with the bold assurance, that unless the succors which were prayed for by his country were promptly accorded, the sword which he then wore at his side as that of an ally of his majesty, would soon, in all probability, be of necessity drawn against him, as that of a subject of Great Britain.

The proceeding, however against rule and precedent, was equally electrical in its effect and beneficial in result. Louis is described as being greatly confused for the moment, but quickly recovering himself, he replied briefly, and graciously received the memorial. The impression made upon the king by the bold young minister was highly favorable, and he distinguished him by his notice, presenting him, when about to leave France, with a magnificent snuff box encircled with diamonds, and surmounted with his own miniature, similarly enriched. This precious gift, valued at a thousand guineas, is still in the possession of the family.

Vergennes was now moved promptly in the right direction. The prayer of the petition was granted; the munitions and money were obtained; and the latter, under the judicious financiering of Robert Morris, enabled Washington to recruit and satisfy his army, and to carry on the war to its triumphant close,

in establishing, as states, the sovereignty and independence of the colonies.

Laurens, with his frank earnestness, resolute zeal
and American directness of purpose, thus achieved a
novel triumph which conveyed a new lesson to the old
world diplomatists of Europe. Having successfully
effected his object, he yielded no time to the fascina-
tions of the French court, but took ship immediately,
and fortunately reached America in safety.

He at once proceeded to resume his active duties
in the field. Great events, contributing largely to
the full close of the grand drama, which through
war led to independence, were culminating to fulfill-
ment. Cornwallis was soon, by a concentration of the
American and French armies under Washington and
Rochambeau, cooped up, and defending himself
stoutly within the narrow trenches of Yorktown.
When the period arrived for assaulting him in his
stronghold, Laurens led one of the storming parties
which carried the British redoubts, and received,
in person, the sword of his captive Cornwallis.

This surrender of the army of Cornwallis entirely
transferred the war to the extreme south, where
Greene held the chief command of the American
forces. Laurens at once hastened to attach himself
to this command. The war in the south had become
one of partisan conflict rather than of grand armies;
and with such chiefs as Marion, Sumter, Pickens,
and others of the same school, actively and incessantly

at work, it was soon evident that the issue, no longer
admitting of a doubt, was simply a question of time.
There were no great cities to capture or defend;
and to conquer one by one, the several scattered
garrisons of the enemy, cut off their supplies
and reinforcements, and force them down to the
seaboard, was the sort of service which, alone was
now required. For such work, Laurens was eminently endowed by his prompt military genius, great
boldness, and celerity of movement. He too, shared
largely in that peculiar talent which has made
famous the names of Marion and Sumter; and, in
this province, he displayed his wonted gallantry and
dash — carrying it sometimes, in the excess of his
zeal, to a desperate extent, which provoked alike the
rebuke and admiration of his contemporaries. His
audacity in the field incurred the reproach of rashness:
but it is matter of question, whether at this period it
did not serve as a wise and useful virtue, in the encouragement of his own troops, and in the corresponding
depression of the enemy. His followers might naturally become dispirited, contending severally against
superior numbers, without clothing or pay, and
frequently without provisions, such only excepted as
they could gather unripened from the fields. In the
interval between his junction with the southern army
and his last battle, he was rarely out of the saddle:
and for a time he cooperated in some of the enterprises of Col. Lee — "Light Horse Harry" — whose

legion grew famous with a reputation wholly its own.
But our space will not suffer us to enter into details
respecting his enterprises, however much they might
serve to illustrate the self-sacrificing daring of his
temper. We must hasten to that painful catastrophe
which punished his temerity — if such it were — and
set its closing seal upon a career, which, wide, various
and in all respects noble, argued gloriously for that
future of performance, which might well be undis-
puted in the case of one still in the very flower of
his youth.

It was in the closing hours of the war, in 1782,
when active operations were almost wholly suspended
on both sides, and when the British were everywhere
making their preparations for leaving the country,
that Laurens, stimulated by his sleepless and almost
feverish zeal and impulse, arose from a sick bed — he
had been suffering from tertian — and taking saddle,
proceeded, with a small force of fifty infantry, a few
matrosses and a single howitzer, to execute one of
those partisan performances which had been his day
by day exercise for a long season. A force of the
British had ascended the Combahee in boats, with the
view of reaping the harvests of rice along that river,
prior to their departure. Laurens resolved on defeat-
ing this object. In fact, the conflicts of the war in the
south, from the termination of the battle of Entaw, had
been chiefly confined to predatory operations on the
part of the British, having this one object in view.

Having been frequently punished severely on these
expeditions by the partisan cavalry and light troops, it
appears that, on the present occasion, they not only
sent forth a larger detachment than usual but resorted
to a more circumspect strategy. They were accordingly better prepared for the whole force led by
Laurens than he had any reason to suspect, and the
neglect of duty, on the part of his scouts and patrols,
enabled the enemy to ascertain his movements while
he remained in comparative ignorance of theirs. It
was known that their barges had ascended the river
to a certain point, and he proceeded to a point below,
called Chehaw, where he hoped to intercept them.
He reached the plantation residence of William Stock,
near Chehaw Point, on the night of the 26th of August
and there rested for the night, with the design to occupy the point at early morning.

But the British, advised of his movements, had
anticipated his purpose. Their barges dropped down
the river under cover of the night, and taking their
station so as to command the point, they landed a
considerable force, which they concealed in the long
grasses and thickets of the place.

It is sad to be told of the gay and graceful manner
in which Laurens spent that evening. In a pleasant
family circle of fine women, he was the courtier, not
the soldier; and the graceful play of society for a few
hours superseded the harsh aspects of deadly struggle.
The conversation passed into pleasant badinage, in the

course of which, we are told, he jestingly proposed
to the ladies that they should be present in a secure
place during the anticipated conflict. Little did he
or they appear to consider for a moment the caprices
of that fate which already had him under doom.

He took horse at early dawn, at the head of his
troops, and the catastrophe was quickly reached. The
enemy rose from his ambush, poured in a destructive
fire, and Laurens was its first victim. He was buried
on the plantation from which he had gone forth with
such an exulting confidence!

Verily, it was a sad close of so brilliant a career;
and that he should perish in an affair of so little consequence, added to the keen and bitter sense of the
public loss. Washington mourned over his fate as
over that of a son. Greene coupled his lament, which
was quite earnest and impassioned, with the reproach
that a life so precious to his country should be
sacrificed for an object of so little significance; and
that, too, at a moment when the struggle was sub-
stantially at an end, and when all the great objects of
the strife had been attained. With them, Hamilton,
Lee, LaFayette, Moultrie, all the master minds of
the revolution, contributed their regrets, and joined
in his eulogium, while the voice of lamentation was
everywhere loud in the land. They all concurred in
their estimate of his great merits as soldier, courtier
and statesman. He had served with, or under, most
of them, and their testimonies were no second hand

tributes, but the fruit of personal association and a
long experience. Numerous anecdotes might be given
illustrating the general feeling and the sympathy of
those officers and soldiers, as well as of the civilians
of the revolution with whom he had won the title
of the Bayard of America.

John Adams writing from Paris to Henry Laurens
shortly after the news of his son's death reached that
capital, says : — " I know not how to mention the me-
lancholy intelligence by this vessel which affects you
so tenderly. I feel for you more than I can or ought
to express. Our country has lost its most promising
character in a manner, however, that was worthy of
her cause. I can say nothing more to you, but that
you have much greater reason to say in this case, as a
Duke of Ormond said of an Earl of Ossory, " I
would not exchange my son for any living son in the
world."[1]   Even personal enemies of Col. Laurens
bore willing testimony to the nobleness of his soul,
and the lofty purity of his chivalry. When in a duel,
he had shot General Charles Lee, because of his
disparaging language concerning Washington, the
wounded man exclaimed : " How handsomely the
young fellow behaved. I could have hugged him!"
His sense of justice, not to say magnanimity, was admirably shown, when promoted by congress, for his

---

[1] Manuscript letter of John Adams to Henry Laurens, Paris, November 6, 1782.

gallantry and public service, but out of the regular
order of promotion in the army, he declined the
commission as a bad precedent, a wrong done to his
comrades, and one which might properly provoke their
jealousy, and occasion disaffection! We may sum up
briefly our estimate of John Laurens, in the language,
with one alteration, which Shakespeare puts into the
mouth of Ophelia when she laments the supposed
overthrow of Hamlet's mind.

> O, what a noble man is here o'erthrown!
> The courtier's, soldier's, scholar's, eye, tongue, sword;
> The expectancy and rose of the fair state,
> The glass of fashion and the mould of form,
> The observ'd of all observers!

Laurens fell on the 27th August, 1782, being then
but twenty-seven years of age. He left a widow and
one young daughter. How these were cared for and
how his public services were acknowledged and
requited, it will suffice to exhibit if we close this
memoir with a letter, never before published, of the
Hon. John C. Hamilton, son of Alexander Hamilton, and a copy of the speech made by the Hon.
Robert Y. Hayne, in the senate of the United
States, on the bill for the relief of the grandson
of Col. John Laurens. These, with the elegiac poem
of Philip Freneau, the poet *par excellence* of the
American Revolution, on the death of Laurens, may
furnish a sufficient close to this brief, but we trust
not wholly unsatisfactory memoir.

The following is the letter of the Hon. John C. Hamilton:

"NEW YORK, *Jan.* 12*th*, 1824.

" Dear Sir:

In the proceedings of the Senate, I yesterday observed the Report of the Committee of Foreign Relations on the Petition of Francis Henderson Jr. In the course of my inquiries I have had an opportunity of forming an opinion of the services of Lieut. Col. Laurens and of the estimation in which he was held by the family of the Commander in chief, which entitles him, beyond all question to the first rank among the young men of the revolution. During his immediate attendance at headquarters he was, with Col. Hamilton always selected to perform the most delicate offices of his station, and was entrusted with Gen. Washington's most secret confidences, and, from the period of the arrival of C^t D'Estaing, until the close of the campaign of 1781, in the communications with the officers of our ally, the aids derived from him were invaluable.

"His military career has left behind him an uninterrupted blaze of glory. Sent forward to R Island, by Gen W. to superintend the conduct of affairs in that quarter until Gen. Greene took the command; to Col. Laurens is principally attributed the reconciliation of D'Estaing, who had been offended by Gen. Sullivan's indiscretion, which

6

excited the most serious apprehensions as to its
effect on our ally. His gallantry on this occasion was
so conspicuous that he received from Congress a vote
of thanks and a tender of a commission of Colonel,
which he declined from delicacy to his brother aids.
At Monmouth where every member of Gen. W's
family seemed to contend, not only for their country
but for their personal reputation, as connected with
their chief, he participated in all the exposure of
the day — and, in the controversy between W. &
Lee which agitated the camp and Congress, such
was his devotion to the former that, late in the
year, he invited Gen. Lee to a rencontre, who,
after receiving a slight wound, made an explanation equally honorable to himself and satisfactory to
his antagonist.

"On the invasion of Georgia in '79, Co¹ L. hastened
to Carolina. Here he was conspicuous in preparing
for the expected invasion. In order to aid the councils
of the State, he was elected a member of their Legisla-
ture where he used every arg^t to call out the militia
and forward the black levies which he had begun to
recruit. On the arrival of Gen. Lincoln, he immediately joined him; was present in the storm of Savannah,
and such was his chivalry, that, after the retreat was
sounded, and the troops had fallen back, he continued
on, in the direction of the enemy's fire until C^t D'Estaing, who was himself wounded, pointed him out to
Lincoln, who ordered him to draw off a detachment in

order to remove him from the field. The misfortune
of that day menacing the most alarming consequences,
Laurens rode express to Philadelphia, in order to urge
succours to the Southern Army. Here he received a
new mark of confidence ; being elected by Congress
Secretary to the Minister at Versailles — a situation
which he peremptorily declined (though sought for
by the most conspicuous names in the country) — in
order to rejoin the army, and was at last induced to
accept, on an intimation " that there was no other
individual on whom the two parties in congress could
unite." Circumstances having occurred to render his
departure on this service unnecessary, he hastened
from Philadelphia and arrived in sufficient season
to take part in the defence of Charleston, where I
presume, he was taken prisoner — (this fact I have to
learn).

" The most important incident, however, of his life
and that having the most immediate relation to the
claim before you, is his mission as Envoy to France in
Feby. 1781. The magnitude of his services on this
occasion are matters of history, but among many interesting incidents connected with this event there is
one which may not be before the public. Vergennes
was opposed to any open interference on our behalf at
the outset of the quarrel, and always continued adverse
to our independence. In this spirit he presented every
obstacle in the way of Col. Laurens negotiation, —
Wearied by these delays L. obtained an interview with

him, and after a warm expostulation, characteristic of his noble spirit, he broke from him — prepared a memorial to the king, and, waiting upon him in the succeeding levée, regardless of the etiquette of the court, handed it to Louis in person. This decisive bearing although it excited great astonishment, was followed by the happiest effects. On the succeeding day the ministers contended with each other in their zeal to promote his views, and he returned here in sufficient season to aid us in a most critical posture of our affairs. (The money obtained by Laurens was deposited in the Bank of N. A. and sustained the financial operations of Mr. Morris until the signature of the provisional treaty). Laurens arrived in Boston, in Sept. 1781, and he immediately joined the army and in the storm of the Redout on the night of the 14th Oct', which was the closing scene of my father's service, L. who, with a body of picked men, was detached by him to take the enemy in reverse and intercept their retreat, entered the works among the foremost and made prisoner the commanding officer. As a compliment to his gallantry and in reference to the capture of Charleston, he with the Viscount De Noailles, was appointed a commissioner to settle the terms of the capitulation.

(Signed)

JOHN C. HAMILTON."

IN THE SENATE.— Remarks of Mr. Hayne, of South Carolina, on the bill for the relief of the grandson of the late Colonel John Laurens.

Mr. Hayne said, that it had been his firm determination to take no part in the discussion of this claim, and to give a silent vote on the several questions which should arise on it. But some erroneous statements had been made which it was in his power to correct, and it had, therefore, become his duty, to give to the senate all the information he possessed on the subject.

The merits of the deceased, Colonel John Laurens, had been brought (he conceived, somewhat improperly) into discussion, on this occasion, inasmuch as the claim of the petitioner was a call on the *justice*, and not on the *bounty*, of the country. As, however, the name of Laurens had been mentioned, he could not, with justice to his own feelings, refrain from adding his feeble tribute of respect for the virtues, and admiration of the character of that distinguished man. He felt that he would be indulged by the senate, when they remembered, that he represented the state which had been honored by giving birth to that illustrious hero, and which had been still more honored in being the scene of his glorious death. Colonel John Laurens, said Mr. Hayne, was the *Bayard* of America. Of him, if of any man who ever lived, it could, with truth, be said, " *he was without fear, and without reproach.*" He brought to the service of his country, a Roman form.

and more than a Roman soul. If you sought for him in the day of battle, he was found at the post of danger; if at any other moment, he was found at the post of duty. The love of his country controlled every other feeling of his heart; it might almost be said, to be that "in which he lived and moved, and had his being." It had been supposed, said Mr. H., that Colonel Laurens was a rash man, wholly reckless of life — who rushed, with the instinct of the lion, on his foe, and who was regardless, because he was insensible to danger. Some countenance, indeed, had been given to this idea by the historians of the day. But Mr. H. was strongly impressed with the belief, that injustice had, in this respect, been done to the character of Laurens, and that his ardent enterprize, and heroic courage, had been mistaken for thoughtless desperation. Laurens possessed a highly cultivated mind. He was a man of thought as well as of action; "as great in council as in high resolve." It is not to be supposed, therefore, that such a man could have been insensible to danger. Mr. H. was satisfied, from facts within his own knowledge, that though Colonel Laurens always felt himself impelled by his noble nature, and a high sense of duty, to seek danger in his country's service, wherever it was to be found, yet he duly estimated the hazards of such conduct, and considered, as probable, the event by which he finally sealed, with his blood, his devotion to his country. When entering on his last campaign, he confided to the care of a friend a precious jewel — the gift of Louis XVIth, with directions how it should be disposed of in the event of his fall. No, sir, said Mr. H., Colonel Laurens was neither insensible to danger, nor indifferent to life. It was only when, to borrow the language of the immortal poet:

> He set *honor* in one eye, and *death* in t'other,
> That he did look on death *indifferently*.

" The field of battle was not the only sphere in which Colonel Laurens displayed great talents, and rare qualities. He was no less able as a negociator, than distinguished as a soldier. At the most critical period of the revolution, congress found it necessary to send to France for succor and support. They sought out Laurens in the camp, and confided to him a special mission to the court of Versailles. His conduct on that mission was as striking and peculiar as it was eminently successful. He stamped his own high character on a transaction unexampled in the whole history of diplomacy. Arrived at the French court, he trampled at once on all the official forms, and in the simple garb of an American soldier, pressed instantly into the presence of the sovereign — eloquently and fearlessly explained the situation of his country, clearly pointed out the duty and interest of France, and demanded assistance. Patriotism and eloquence were signally triumphant — Laurens prevailed. He obtained at once that relief which was, perhaps, essential to the accomplishment of American

Independence, and which if it had not been wholly
denied to the usual course of tardy negociation, might
have come too late to produce the desired effect. Thus
was the work of years accomplished in a few short
weeks. But a few months had elapsed since Laurens
had been seen in the ranks of the American army "in
the thickest of the fight." And now (having in the
meantime twice crossed the Atlantic, and concluded a
most important negociation), he was again on his
native shores, bringing with him immense treasures,
the fruits of his labors, and furnishing pay and clothing to the suffering soldiery. In a few days after his
arrival, he was again found in the camp, marshalling
to glory the soldiers of liberty. Mr. H. said, he
would not attempt to follow him further in his glorious course. We all know that he fell at the head of
his troops gallantly fighting for the liberties of his
country, and the rights of mankind. It is delightful,
said Mr. H., to reflect that he fell " in the last of our
fields," as if Providence, who had preserved him
through so many perils, had permitted his career to
be closed only when there were no more battles to be
won. It will hardly be believed by posterity, that the
hero who filled so large a space in the annals of his
country, died in his youth, not having yet attained his
twenty-seventh year.

"As nearly connected with this subject, said Mr. H.,
it is worthy of remark, that Col. Laurens was the
purest and most disinterested of human beings. His

political creed was, that in the hour of calamity, the
life and fortune of the citizen is the property of his
country, and that his services should be rendered gra-
tuitously. Laurens received no pay — kept no private
accounts, and, most certainly, never intended to demand, nor would have consented to receive, any
compensation for his invaluable services, military and
diplomatic. It was in the same spirit, that on one occasion, he declined a commission in the army, tendered
him as a reward for his gallantry; not, assuredly, from
insensibility to its value (for military glory was the idol
of his soul, and promotion the very reward for which
his heart panted), but because, as he himself declared,
his promotion might give offence to older officers;
and thus be injurious to the public service. Mr. H.
said, he knew not how better to combine in one view,
the various traits which marked the character of John
Laurens, than by adopting the elegant language of the
American historian: "Nature had adorned him with
a profusion of her choicest gifts, to which education
had added its most useful as well as its most elegant
improvements. Acting from the most honorable
principles — uniting the bravery and other talents of
the great officer, with the knowledge of a complete
soldier, and the engaging manners of a well bred gentleman — he was the idol of his country — the glory
of the army, and the ornament of human nature."

"It was such a man, said Mr. H., as he had
described — so gallant in war, so happy in negocia-

7

tion, and whose good fortune it was to have rendered such immense services to his country, that at the end of the revolution, closed his glorious life, by a still more glorious death. Cut down in the midst of all his prospects, he left an infant child, an orphan daughter; and had that child been left destitute and friendless, what would the American nation have done? What ought they to have done? Sir, they would have imitated Rome, in the best, the most virtuous days of that republic. They would have adopted that orphan. She would have become the child of the republic, which would have cherished and protected her — reared her up to honor and usefulness, and finally have bestowed on her " a suitable dowry in marriage." But such was fortunately not her destitute condition. She was left to the paternal care of her venerable grandfather, a man of high character, of large fortune, and to whom his deceased son had been dearer than his own life.

" It was supposed to be proper to apply to congress in behalf of the orphan, for the payment of the salary to which her father was entitled as a military officer, and a foreign minister. All that was asked was granted; the pay was adjusted — the account settled, and the money received and applied to the use of the child. At a subsequent period she was married in England to the petitioner, who, in the right of his wife, became entitled to receive a considerable fortune, composed of the money granted by congress, and the bequest of her grandfather. In this situation matters have remained for upwards of thirty years, when the petitioner discovers, that in the adjustment of Col. Laurens' account, other claims might have been introduced; and he comes here in his own right, and asks not only for the corrections of errors in the settlement, but also for interest for forty years on the whole amount — interest, which is not the practice of this government to allow. Now, sir, if the daughter of Col. Laurens was in pecuniary distress, and were to come here, and ask of your liberality, assistance and support, it would become this house — it would be worthy of the nation to extend the hand of kindness, and generously to bestow any sum of money necessary for her relief. It ought not, however, in such a case, to be presented, in the shape of a demand, for interest on an account, but the lasting gratitude due for the services of the father, ought to be the foundation of a liberal donation to the child.

"But the parties to this petition make no appeal. It is a simple demand by the legal representative, for the settlement of an account, to which, therefore, the usual rules ought to be applied. No complaint is made of pecuniary distress; no appeal has been made or could be made, with any propriety, to your sympathies. Let justice, then, be done; but let the bounty of the country be reserved for a more suitable occasion. With respect to the claim of interest, on the ground that all the parties have constantly resided

in England, Mr. H. said, the honorable chairman of
the committee was mistaken, in point of fact; and this
was one of the errors which Mr. H. had risen to correct. The petitioner was in this country upwards
of twenty years ago; had been here on one or two
occasions since, and had resided in America for
several years past. Interest could not be claimed on
that ground.

"It only remains, then, said Mr. H., to enquire what
does justice require at our hands, in this case? It is
alleged by the petitioner, that certain errors exist in
the settlement of Col. Laurens' account, under the
resolutions of congress of 1784. The respectable committee to whom the subject has been referred, have
reported that in their opinion the allegation has been
supported by proof. With that report, Mr. H. was
disposed to rest satisfied; more especially, as it
appeared to him, from the examination he had been
enabled to make, that there were good grounds for that
opinion. It might, indeed, be objected, by persons
disposed to be over scrupulous, that the account having been long settled, every presumption ought to be
indulged against the claim. But he thought that
would be applying a rule too technical, and much too
rigid for such a case; more especially, as the items
of which the claim was composed, could be easily
brought to the test of a rigid examination. It is
alleged by the petitioner, that Col. Laurens was not
allowed his expenses, as a foreign minister, but only

the usual salary; and it is insisted, that it was the
universal practice to allow these expenses, in lieu of
the outfit, which has since been established by law.
Both of these facts are susceptible of the clearest
proof. The account which was settled, shews plainly,
say the committee, that no allowance was made for
expenses; and that it was then usual to allow these
expenses, is manifest from the journals and documents
submitted. The committee have informed us that
the sum reported is in exact proportion to that allowed
to Silas Deane and other foreign ministers, on the
same account. The other items are of small amount,
and from the statements of the chairman, seem to be
equally satisfactorily proved. The amount of these
items ought therefore to be paid; but in the shape in
which this claim was now presented, Mr. H. thought
without interest. The United States did not in
general allow interest, and he saw no sufficient reason to make this case an exception to the rule. Had
the petitioner insisted on the payment of the amount
of the claim to himself, and for his own use, by virtue
of his marital rights, Mr. H. said he would have felt
great reluctance in complying with that demand.
But he had wisely consented that the amount should
be paid to his son, the only grandchild of Col. John
Laurens; and believing that his mother was suitably
provided for, and that the best direction the money
could possibly take, was to make a provision for that
young man, at the commencement of his career in

life, Mr. H. was satisfied with the bill, as reported by the committee, and should give it his vote.

" Mr. Hayne said he was happy in being able to add that he believed the grandson to be a respectable young man, who was preparing himself for the practice of an honorable profession in the country; and he indulged the hope that he would become a valuable citizen, and prove himself worthy of his ancestors."

LINES

ON THE DEATH OF COLONEL LAURENS.

BY PHILIP FRENEAU.

Since on her plains this generous chief expir'd,
Whom sages honour'd and whom France admir'd;
Does Fame no statues to his memory raise,
Nor swells one column to record his praise
Where her palmetto shades the adjacent deeps,
Affection sighs, and Carolina weeps!

Thou, who shalt stray where death this chief confines,
Revere the patriot, subject of these lines:
Not from the dust the muse transcribes his name,
And more than marble shall declare his fame
Where scenes more glorious his great soul engage,
Confest thrice worthy in that closing page
When conquering Time to dark oblivion calls,
The marble totters, and the column falls.

LAURENS! thy tomb while kindred hands adorn,
Let northern muses, too, inscribe your urn.—
Of all, whose names on death's black list appear,
No chief, that perish'd, claim'd more grief sincere,
Not one, Columbia, that thy bosom bore,
More tears commanded, or deserv'd them more!—
Grief at his tomb shall heave the unwearied sigh,
And honour lift the mantle to her eye:
Fame thro' the world his patriot name shall spread,
By heroes envied and by monarchs read:

Just, generous, brave — to each true heart allied :
The Briton's terror, and his country's pride ;
For him the tears of war-worn soldiers ran,
The friend of freedom, and the friend of man.

   Then what is death, compar'd with such a tomb,
Where honour fades not, and fair virtues bloom,
When silent grief on every face appears,
The tender tribute of a nation's tears ;
Ah ! what is death, when deeds like his thus claim
The brave man's homage, and immortal fame !

CORRESPONDENCE OF JOHN LAURENS.

HEAD QUARTERS, near the Cross Roads,
13th August, 1777.

My Dear Father:

We moved to this place on the 10th inst. Here we received the account from Synnepuxent, and remain at fault till some more particular accomts of the motions of the enemy enable me to judge of their designs. In the meantime our soldiers are recruiting in a plentiful country, as well as strong drink and women will permit them.

These impediments, however, to their laying in a stock of good health are not so general as might be expected in an army situated as ours is.

The men are exercised in smaller or greater numbers every day. The country people bring in a plenty of vegetables, &c.—and we hear very few complaints from those immediately about us of the violations of private property. We are all anxious to hear something that will give us employment of a different kind

8

from that which we have at present.   My best regards
to all our friends, and I remain ever

Your most affectionate

JOHN LAURENS.

I have no prospect yet of horses or servant.
The Honble Henry Laurens, Esq.,
    at Mrs. Aries, Market street, near 4th street.

———

HEAD QUARTERS, 21*st August*, 1777.

My Dear Father:

As we shall probably move to-morrow, I write to
inform you that I must be obliged to use your horses
and servant farther on — there having been no possibility of supplying myself with these articles here.
Shrewsberry says his hat was violently taken from
him by some soldiers, as he was carrying his horses
to water.   If James will be so good as to send him
his old laced hat by the bearer, I hope he will take
better care of it.

If the enemy have a design upon Charles Town
which does not so clearly appear to me as it does
to most people, I hope we shall ruin the northern
branch of their army, and that however they may
for a while distress an individual state, their efforts
against the general confederacy will be less likely to

succeed than ever. I commend myself to your love
and remain

Your ever affectionate

JOHN LAURENS.

The Honble Henry Laurens, Esq., at Mrs. Aries,
  Market street near 4th St., Philadelphia.

My Dear Father :

I have just a minute to beg the favor of you to send
my watch by Col. Tilghman : Messrs. Pinckney
and Horry arriv'd here yesterday, but they could not
inform me certainly whether you had employ'd Hunt
to buy me a horse. I am exceedingly in want of a
vigorous steed that can gallop and leap well, not
younger than four, but I would rather have him of
six or seven years of age. Your kindness will excuse
my hurry and the trouble I give. The gentlemen
above mention'd gave me pleasure in informing me
that you were well. Col. Tilghman will answer
any questions respecting the motions of the enemy
and our own.

Your affectionate

JOHN LAURENS.

30th Aug^t, 1777.
The Honble Henry Laurens, Esqr.

HEAD QUARTERS, near Potts Grove,
26th Septem., 1777.

My Dear Father:

M^r. Forsyth, the bearer of this, takes charge of four packets for you, two of which I received yesterday and two to-day. He has likewise two other packets for other members of Congress, one of them directed to your care. I have desired him in case of your removal from Reading to call on General Mifflin who will have the letters forwarded. We shall move towards Philadelphia to-day, as the weather is fair and our reinforcements are at some distance below, ready to fall in with us. Yesterday, the enemy halted at Chestnut Hill, not far from Germantown, and there was a cannonading heard in the morning down the river. I am your most affectionate

JOHN LAURENS.

The Honble Henry Laurens, Esqr., Reading.

HEAD QUARTERS, WAMPOLES, 15th October, 1777.

When an opportunity offers, however little I have to communicate, my desire of conversing with you leads me to take up the pen at all events even tho' the impossibility of giving you information upon public and more interesting objects should confine me to the old family style of ' I continue in good health as I hope you do,' etc.

The northern intelligence which was accidentally
handed to us yesterday, but which you no doubt have
received in proper form, is subject matter for con-
gratulation.

I beg leave to felicitate you upon the victory gained
over the haughty Burgoyne, a victory which derives
much of its importance from the critical time in which
it happened. It was announced to the American
prisoners in Howe's possession by a flag that happened
to be going in yesterday. After all my good intentions
I am obliged to break off abruptly, as M^r. Harrison
the bearer hurries me, and my letter will serve only
to inclose one left here yesterday for Col. Pinckney.

Yours affection^y

JOHN LAURENS.

The Honble Henry Laurens Esqr, York,
    favor of Col^o Harrison.

1 Lt Gen.
2 Major Generals
7 Brig.
2 Eng ⎫
1 Irish ⎬ Noblem.
A qty of Clothing.
5000 Privats
15000 Stand Arms
40 Brass Cann^n

The above in the hand writing of Henry Laurens is
endorsed on the back of the letter dated 15th October,
1777.

HEAD QUARTERS — Whitemarsh Camp,
5th November, 1777.

My Dear Father :

In our present camp form'd of two commanding hills, whose front and flanks bid defiance to assailants, additionally secured by a very strong advanced post, and well supplied with every necessary, we wait the arrival of reinforcements from the north,— a part of which is on its march and will soon arrive. What we are to do when reinforced depends upon circumstances.

If our forts hold out and we do our duty, Gen' Howe will find himself in a situation which will require the utmost exertions of military talents to bring him off with honor. He has already experienced some difficulty in subsisting his troops and Tory adherents; perhaps he might have been reduced to the necessity of retreating, if there had been proper concert in the proceedings of our fleet and garrison. The enemy's boats pass and repass at night, carry supplies from the shipping to the town, and meet with no interruption. The cannon of the fort cannot be brought to bear upon them; random firing would be a waste of precious ammunition. The galleys alone can be opposed to their passage, which has been hitherto effected between Province Island and Fort Mifflin, under cover of darkness. What this inactivity of the galleys is owing to is unknown; some attribute it to the jealousy which commonly subsists between the officers of the naval and land service—a vitious spirit which should not be known in Republics. However I have reason to believe that this communication will be cut off for the future.

The Reinforcements for this army are arrived at Red-bank — the intended addition has been made to the two garrisons, and the remainder will be posted in a proper situation for falling on the rear of any storming party, or annoying the enemy in any more formal attack on Red-bank. This morning a heavy cannonading was heard from below and continued till afternoon; from the top of Chew's house in German Town to which place the General took a ride this morning, we could discover nothing more than thick clouds of smoak, and the masts of two vessels, the weather being very hazy.

This days Philadelphia paper contains Genl Burgoyne's Letter to Sr Wm Howe: as I cannot send you the paper itself I copy the letter —

Copy of a Letter, &c., brought by Lieut. Valancy of the 62d.

ALBANY, *Octob.* 20*th.*

" Sir :

In conformity to my orders — to proceed by the most vigorous exertions to Albany, I pass'd the Hudson's River at Saratoga on the 13th September.

" No exertions have been left untried. The army under my command has fought twice against great

superiority of numbers. The first action was on the
19th Septem. when after four hours sharp conflict,
we remain'd masters of the field of battle. The 2d
action (on the 7th October) was not so successful and
ended with a storm upon two parts of our intrench-
ments, the one defended by Lieut. Col. Breyman who
was kill'd upon the spot, and the post was lost, the
other defended by Lord Balcarras at the head of the
British Light Infantry who repulsed the enemy with
great loss. The army afterwards made good their
retreat to the heights of Saratoga, unable to proceed
farther, the enemy having possession of all the fords
and the passes on the east side of Hudson's River.
The army waited the chances of events and offer'd
themselves to the attack of the enemy 'till the 13th
inst — when only three days provision at short allowance remained. At that time the last hope of timely
assistance being exhausted, my numbers reduced by
past actions to three thousand five hundred fighting
men, of which about nineteen hundred alone were
British; invested by the enemys troops to the
amount of sixteen thousand men; I was induced by
the general concurrence and advice of the General,
Field officers and Captains commanding Corps, to
open a Treaty with Major Gen¹ Gates. Your
Excellency will observe by the papers transmitted
herewith, the disagreeable prospect that attended the
first overtures. The army determined to die to a
man, rather than submit to terms repugnant to

national and personal honor. I trust you will think
the Treaty inclosed consistent with both.

I am with the greatest respect and attachment,

Sir, &c.,

(Signed),   J. BURGOYNE."

The first overtures alluded to in the above letter.

1st. General Burgoyne's army being exceedingly
reduced by repeated defeats, by desertion, sickness,
&c., — their provisions exhausted, their military stores,
tents and baggage taken or destroyed, their retreat
cut off and their camp invested, they can only be allowed to surrender prisoners of war.

Answer. Lieut. Gen¹ Burgoyne's army, however
reduced, will never admit that their retreat is cut
off, while they have arms in their hands.

2. The officers and soldiers may keep the baggage
belonging to them.   The generals of the United
States never permit individuals to be pillaged.

3. The troops under his excell⁷ Gen¹ Burgoyne will
be conducted by the most convenient route to N. England, marching by easy marches, and sufficiently provided for by the way.

4th. The officers will be admitted on parole, may
wear their side arms, and will be treated with the
liberality customary in Europe, so long as they by
proper behaviour continue to deserve it; but those
who are apprehended having broke their parole (as

9

some British officers have done) must expect to be closely confined.

Answer. There being no officer in this army, under or capable of being under the description of breaking parole, this article needs no answer.

5th. All public stores, artillery, arms, ammunition, carriages, horses, &ca., must be deliver'd to Commissaries appointed to recieve them.

Answer. All public stores may be deliver'd — arms excepted.

6th. These terms being agreed to and sign'd, the troops under His Excellys Gen¹ Burgoynes command may be drawn up in their encampment, where they will be order'd to ground their arms, and may be thereupon march'd to the river side, to be pass'd over in their way towards Bennington.

Answer. This article is inadmissible in any extremity; sooner than this army will consent to ground their arms in their encampment, they will rush on the enemy determined to take no quarter.

October 14th, 1777.

These overtures being rejected the present Convention took place.

In this paper are continued the proclamations on promising 200 Acres of Land to each non commisioned officer, and 50 to each private who shall serve in the Provincial Corps now raising — the other marking the 1st day of December next as the last term of pardon for deserters from His Majesty's services. The most remarkable advertisements are — " Wanted immediately an additional number of able bodied men, to serve on the city nightly parole, those desirous of serving are to apply to J. Delaplane Constable of the watch. Wanted, a number of hands to cut wood during the winter season, for the use of the army — good encouragement will be given &ca.

The inhabitants of Philadelphia, Germantown and the country about are desired to make a return of the number of horses, waggons, teams and carts in their possession.

Those that choose to hire their waggons by the day, shall be paid the customary price and those who conceal their waggons, and do not make returns as above, will have them seized.

NB. A number of men wanted to drive waggons — their pay shall be three shillings N. York Currency and provisions found them."

The day before yesterday, Mr Crouch and another gentleman pass'd thro' camp in their way from the eastward to Charles Town. They said they intended to continue their journey early the next morning. I was out till late dinner time with the General, was busy after dinner, and consequently had but little time for private affairs — however, I accomplished a letter to Mrs Laurens which I enclosed to Mr Gervais to be forwarded, giving him for his pains as much news as

I could recollect and commit hastily to paper, and
what will be a treasure to him as a Newsmonger,
Humphrey's Gazette of the 25th. I expected to have
been able to procure another for you, but have been
disappointed.

The light manner in which Count Donops affair is
related.— Sr Wm Howe's Kitean harangue to such
he would delude into the loyal corps of which he has
reserved to himself the Coloneley — and other little
anecdotes, may make it acceptable even a day or
two hence, if you have not already seen it, and in
that time I may get it from some one whose curiosity
and that of his circle is satisfied or called off to something more recent.

A day or two ago, Capt Lee of the light horse with
twelve of his troops, dispersed a foraging party on
the other side Schuylkill, took a Captain of the
Queen's Rangers (this is the name given to the new
levies of provincial troops), and seven privates, two of
whom were marines.— He gives us intelligence that
Genl Howe's first Aid de Camp is embarked for
England and that his principal business is to solicit
speedy and large reinforcements. This will be
delivered to you by a Baron Frey, who brought a
letter of recommendation from Doctor Franklin to
the General, and is carrying one to Mr Morris. He
left France in August, at which time he says it was
the serious opinion of people in France that the Court
of G. Britain had obtained 30,000 Russians.

Between copying and composing I have inked a great deal of paper, and it begins to be time for me to join in the concert of my snoring companions, who are extended before the fire in the style which we practiced in the interior parts of So. Carolina. I wish you as sound sleep with the cares of state as I am likely to have, and continue in every circumstance and situation my dear father.

Your most dutiful
JOHN LAURENS.

The Honble Henry Laurens, Esqr.

HEAD QUARTERS, 7th November, 1777.

I had the pleasure of writing to you yesterday by Col° Morgan, and the day before by Baron Frey, a stranger lately arrived from France who is gone to offer his service to Congress. The cannonading heard day before yesterday was between the Somerset 64 Gun Ship, the Roebuck and some other vessel on the one part, and our row-gallies seconded by a two gun battery on the other — the affair was as follows:

The above mentioned vessels advanced towards our chevaux de frise — Genl Varnum had thrown up a fascine battery on a commanding piece of ground below Red-bank, and order'd an eighteen pounder and a twelve pounder to be moved into it. The eighteen pounder was overset in its way, which accident prevented its arrival before two o'clock. In

the intermediate time, however, the piece of twelve,
was well employed — the ships dropped down to the
distance of a mile and a half from the battery, and
the Somerset ran aground, in which situation she
underwent a constant Fire from the Battery, which
Gen¹ Varnum thinks must have injur'd her exceedingly. She made several signals of distress, upon
which our Commodore with a great force advanced
towards her and made a dreadful but ineffectual
roaring with his cannon — the Roebuck, with the third
vessel whose name I dont recollect and a galley,
brought their bow guns to bear on our fleet and
kept them at a respectful distance. The flood made,
and the Somerset moved slowly off under cover of the
other ships. — She received farewell salutes from the
battery as long as she continued within reach.

Our anxiety had been raised in camp, by a report
that a heavy firing of musquetry had been heard for a
considerable time on the evening of the same day —
it turns out to be nothing more than a few single
guns which Potter's militia and the enemy's detachment on Province Island make a practice of firing
at each other without com⁶ to any action. Four
deserters from the enemy brought in this morning, say
that the militia men call'd to the British soldiers and
invited them to go over, promising them beef and
flour — the red-coats in return ask'd them to come
and partake of their salt — that from raillery they
proceeded to abuse and at length to discharging

their pieces at each other, without any other effect as
far as they know than wounding a Hessian yager.

There have been several women from Ph^a within
two days past, who have applied for leave to pass into
the country — declaring that unless this indulgence
be granted to them, they must inevitably starve.
Our humane General says he will grant their request
upon condition that they do not return into the city,
and I believe directions are given for that purpose to
the officers commanding sub-posts, who have hitherto
stopt them.

Rubenhaupt, the Dutch general who conducted the
celebrated siege of Grave, shielded by national phlegm
against any impression from female and infantine distress, rudely sent back into the town crowds of
women and children, who presented themselves in his
camp to entreat that he would deliver them from the
horrors of famine by suffering them to pass his lines.

The polite and gallant Prince of Condé, upon a
similar application, when he was particularly called
upon not to act inconsistently with the amiable
characteristic of his countrymen — the women of the
besieged town who petitioned his leave to quit it,
saying "they were persuaded a *French* Nobleman
could not be so impolite as to reject the prayer of
unfortunate ladies —" dexterously parried this artful
address to his feelings as a Frenchman, by replying
that "he could not consent to deprive himself of the
most desirable part of his conquest."

I write this to go by James, who came to Head Quarters this morning to see me and take my commands. I happen'd to be out with the General when he arrived, and did not know of his being here 'till after dinner, which according to our late hour, made it near evening — and as I had a second ride to take I detained him for the rest of the day. Mrs. Hartley is too far from camp for me to pay her my respects. If James returns that way, I will write her a note of thanks for her care of your letter of 26th Octob^r which I received yesterday.

8th. His Excellency detains James in order to write by him to Congress — I congratulate you, upon your succession to the Presidentship, tho' we shall not know you in that capacity at Head Quarters 'till you are announced.

Permit me to say, that I have the honour to be with as much respect for your public station, as any citizen in the United States, and with an increasing flow of filial affection.

Your dutiful son,

JOHN LAURENS.

I wrote yesterday to St. Mary Axe, under cover to Babut and Labouchere, by way of New Orleans, and committed my packet to the care of Col° Morgan.

Since writing as above, I have received your kind favor of the 4th.

The Hon'ble Henry Laurens, Esq.

HEAD QUARTERS, 9ᵗʰ *November*, 1777.

My Dear Father:

Colonel du Portail's visit to Congress gives me an opportunity of relating some little transactions which serve by way of interlude to the grand acts of the military drama. Capt. Craig of Moylan's Light Dragoons, with sixteen horsemen surprised one of the enemy's patrols this morning, consisting of seven horse and seven grenadiers and took the whole party prisoners without a stroke on either side. The same officer informs us this afternoon from authority which he thinks good, that fifteen of the enemy's provision boats have fall'n into our hands.

We have received accounts from different persons that one of their floating batteries was sunk in launching.

From the preparations made and every account obtained from deserters, spies, &c., we have reason to expect every day a pow'rful attack on Fort Mifflin. General Varnum has reinforced the garrison from his brigade, and such a disposition is made of our naval and land force in that quarter as will make a greater sacrifice the price of success, than I think Mr Howe in his present circumstances can afford. This evening, Capt Nichols of the Eagle packet with the Capt of an armed sloop, were brought to Head Quarters — they were made prisoners by a detachment from Capt Lee's troop, and as Nichols mentioned his being acquainted with some gentlemen of Carolina,

10

Capt Lee gave him a recommendatory letter to me. The honest seaman, tho' he says his vessel was order'd to be in readiness for sailing at a moment's warning, seems to be affected by his misfortune and expresses as hearty rejoicing at the welfare of President Laurens as if he were a loyal subject to his master. He says that Pond was on shore with him and narrowly escaped accompanying him hither.

I am sorry to deduct from your pleasure by striking out the story of the provision boats. Upon reading Genl Varnum's letter of yesterday, I find mention of a convoy being driven back by our gallies; the delay of their arrival has probably given room to conjecture in Philadelphia that they had been taken.

10th. I have just return'd from an early walk to an eminence in front of the camp, where I had been listening to the tremendous, tho' distant roaring of cannon. It is probable that this infernal noise is only a prelude to the more dangerous closer fight which has been so long meditated by the British and which both parties are prepared for.

Will you be so kind as to tell me the orthography of galley, whether it be as already written, or thus gally.

Your most affectionate

JOHN LAURENS.

The Honble Henry Laurens, Esq.,
   President of Congress, York.

HEAD QUARTERS, 14th *Novem.*, 1777.

My Dear Father:

Since I had the pleasure of writing to you by Baron Frey, and the Chevalier du Portail, the siege of Fort Mifflin has been continued with great vigour and the new batteries open'd by the enemy on the 10th have thrown their 24 and 32 pounders with great success. A considerable breach was made on the 11th in the masonry of the fort, many palisades were level'd, the block houses almost ruin'd, several cannon dismounted, and a valuable artillery officer kill'd. In these circumstances the commanding officer Lieut. Col. Smith thought proper to consult with Brigadier Genl Varnum who is stationed at Woodberry near Fort Mercer on Red Bank, upon the propriety of evacuating the post. It was determined that the superfluous cannon, provisions and artillery stores should be removed and that a show of defence should be kept up as long as possible. The commander in chief considering the importance of this place, which if it should fall into the enemy's hands would enable them to annoy our fleet and even drive it from the defence of the chevaux de frise, at first gave positive orders to maintain it at all events. These, however, were changed for discretionary orders in consequence of the great injury which the works had sustained. On the night of the 11th the enemy's fire interrupted the repairs of the fort. Three of

their small vessels pass'd between Province Island
and the fort to the mouth of the Schuylkil. On the
12th there was a great firing and two eighteen
pounders dismounted. At night the enemy threw
shells and the garrison was alarmed by thirty of their
boats. On the 13th they open'd a new battery; our
block houses were destroyed; each day there were a
few kill'd and wounded. The garrison exhausted by
watching labour and ill health have been relieved.
The enemy have not been tempted by the success of
their batteries to storm a small number of men who
maintained their ground in the ruins of the fort.
I certainly think it practicable by nocturnal labours
to complete a work which will bid defiance to storm,
and cover the garrison from their 32 pounders. The
engineer who is on the spot, Major Fleury, a Frenchman, will do every thing that can be done. His zeal
and talents recommend him to public notice. To
night the enemy have renewed their firing.

13th. Nothing like a storm yet from the detachment on Province Island. They content themselves
with battering by day, and interrupting as much as
they can our fatigue parties at night by firing from
time to time — in which the moonlight is serviceable
to them.

14th. Early this morning a floating battery armed
with two heavy cannon was discover'd near the shore
of Province Island. The new commandant at Fort
Mifflin thinks the post tenable in spite of the enemy's

land and water batteries. The Engineer Fleury says if he is supplied from Red Bank with fascines, gabions, earth and fatigue-men, he will repair as much as possible each night the havoc made by day. What he will principally aim at will be the construction of some flanked work (shaped according to circumstances) which in case the block houses sh^d be irreparably lost, may enable the garrison to resist a storm.

15. There has been firing in the course of the day and some scatter'd guns in the evening.

16. Every account given by persons of different sexes and ages who have left Philadelphia agrees in these points, that the inhabitants are exceedingly distressed for want of provision. Officers and soldiers humbled by the unexpected resistance of the forts, begin to express great anxiety on account of their present situation — that our unhappy prisoners are treated with a barbarity which I think the Britons can only venture to be guilty of, because they persuade themselves the relation of it will not be believed in the present refined age.

Gentlemen return'd from reconnoitering on the other side of Schuylkil say that the Continental flag was flying at Fort Mifflin yesterday evening,— that the enemy by lightering a frigate of her guns had towed her through a shallow channel between Hog Island and Province Island.

With this you will receive a Philadelphia paper

and a printed handbill which is one of a great number
lately found in a chest at East Town. The direction
of the chest is rubb'd off and there were no manuscripts within by which the owner could be discover'd;
each handbill was inscribed with the address which
you see on this. Capt Robinson calls for my letter.
Adieu my dear Father.

JOHN LAURENS.

I had closed my letter persuaded that Fort Mifflin
was still ours, when an officer from Red Bank enter'd
with Genl Varnum's dispatches. The enemy's fire
yesterday was universal. Ships, batteries, land and
water, one of the latter stationed near the fort threw
in hand grenades — our brave garrison suffer'd considerably — some of our best officers wounded — and
Genl Varnum, I suppose, ordered the fort to be
evacuated last night. The fort has done infinitely
more than was expected of it, and we must repair its
loss.

HEAD QUARTERS, 18th Novem., 1777.

My Dear Father:

Your kind letter of the 12th, concluded on the 15th,
has been deliver'd to me barely time enough to run it
over.

The express is to be sent back immediately with
dispatches that were ready, so that I shall have but
few moments allowed me for writing to you. The

little innovation in the epithet applied to Gen¹ Howe's oration, I took the liberty of forming from Kite, a character in the comedy of the Recruiting Officer, and meant to draw a parallel between the sergeant's harangue and that of the General — but upon recollection I believe I have done the former an injustice — who confined his promises to more practicable things. I shall not now have time to give you my dear Father a particular account of the progress of the besiegers and persevering defence of our brave garrison, to the time when perpetual hail of musquetry and hand grenades from the round tops of the Empress of Russia, an East Indiaman cut down and converted into a floating battery of 18 twenty-four pounders, made it impossible for men to do any thing more in the fort than sacrifice themselves unrevenged. I hate to blame without sure grounds; but as far as I can judge at this distance, the naval department has been deficient in its duty. The Commodore is brave, but has no command. The questions now are — can we prevent the enemy's raising the chevaux de frise by keeping possession of Red Bank or Fort Mercer — if the enemy should effect a lodgment on Mud Island can our fleet maintain its present position? Is it not possible to take the Empress of Russia, and sink an obstruction in the channel thro' which she pass'd? I say yes to them all, except the second — and the enemy's lodgmᵗ may be prevented.

You, my dear father will call me a presumptuous

young man, especially when you hear that three general officers are gone to investigate these points on the spot. Pardon the manner of my letter, in consideration that I have been endeavouring to satisfy the problem which requires the most written in the least given time. Chagrined at the necessity of taking leave so abruptly, I console myself with the prospect of writing more deliberately in a day or two.

Your most affectionate

JOHN LAURENS.

The Honble Henry Laurens, Esqr.,
    President of Congress, York.

HEAD QUARTERS, 26th Novem., 1777.

My Dear Father:

Mr Boudinot, commissary of prisoners informs me that he intends for York to morrow, and if I understand him right, wishes that I would give him a letter of introduction to you. He is a sensible man and attentive to the duties of his office.

Your kind letter of the 23^d announces a very acceptable reinforcement of linnen for which I am exceedingly obliged to you — the boots will come in good time — those which I wear at present are in good condition, but where they undergo such hard duty as they do in the service of an aide de camp, a relief is necessary. The gloves are not so indispensible, I have discover'd an old pair which have been washed and serve me with reparation; the woolen ones however will be an exceeding good reserve.

I believe your question relative to the proceedings of the enemy since the evacuation of Fort Mifflin, has been answered in one of my former letters.

Troops from Province Island immediately possess'd themselves of the ruin'd wall and palisades, and threw up a battery. At the evacuation of Fort Mercer a quantity of powder was fired with intention to blow up the magazine and ruin the works — however, it had but little effect, and the destruction was completed by the enemy.

Gen¹ Greene had prepared to give Lᵈ Cornwallis battle, when he was call'd off by a grand scheme which was in agitation the day before yesterday. An attack was meditated on the enemy's lines; a proper disposition was plann'd for attacking their redoubts vigorously in front, while Greene's detachment embark'd in boats should fall down the river land in the city and charge the enemy in their rear. A cannonade from an eminence on the west side of Schuylkil was to second these attacks and Potter's Militia were to make a show at the bridge. Some were clearly for it and some clearly against it; both parties ignorant at the same time of the strength of the works. Our Commander in chief wishing ardently to gratify the public expectation by making an attack upon the enemy — yet preferring at the same time a loss of popularity to engaging in an enterprise which he could

11

not justify to his own conscience and the more respectable part of his constituents, went yesterday to view the works. A clear sunshine favoured our observations: we saw redoubts of a very respectable profit, faced with plank, formidably fraised, and the intervals between them closed with an abbatis unusually strong. General du Portail declared that in such works with five thousand men he would bid defiance to any force that should be brought against him. I was led into all the history which I must beg my dear father may be very discreet — but now no secret — however my friends in Carolina may talk of things they know without quotation — I know my few friends there are also discreet, between ourselves — in order to account for Gen¹ Greene's not marching to L⁴ Cornwallis — as every man of experience and judgment thinks it would be madness with our force to make an attempt on the enemy in their present situation.

It follows that in order to guard against L⁴ Cornwallis's being suddenly recall'd, and the enemy's marching with their whole force against our army, weakened by a considerable detachment, we should withdraw Gen¹ Greene from the Jerseys — and a courier has been accordingly dispatched for that purpose. When the junction is form'd we shall probably march to some place where the troops may be cover'd from the inclemency of the season, and be within distance for annoying the enemy's shipping and cutting off any detachments which they may have occasion to make. A position on the other side of Schuylkil would unite these two advantages and have the additional ones of being in a more plentiful country for forage, &ca., and reducing the enemy to the passage of a bridge in case they should attempt a sudden attack upon us. German Town would cover a great many troops, but it would require strong works to secure it, and is within surprising distance.

I was going to speak privately of several public matters, but the horses are order'd, and what I write must be dispatched hastily. The promotion of Col. Wilkinson to the rank of Brigad[r] General has given universal disgust in the corps of Continental officers. If he had signalized himself, say many of them, by any remarkable service, we should have applauded Congress for bestowing a well merited reward; but we think there is a degradation of rank and an injustice done to senior and more distinguished officers, when a man is so extraordinarily advanced for riding post with good news. Let Congress reward him with a good horse for his speed, but consecrate rank to merit of another kind.

This matter is likely to produce many resignations in the line of colonels. Rank has likewise been vilified by the indiscriminate distribution of it. Waggon masters, regimental quarter masters, &ca., have had titles which cease to be honorable when possessed by such personages.

I had some other things to say — but I believe I

shall be better employed for the present in sending you such extracts as I shall have time to cull from the last Philadelphia paper. I give you the paragraphs quoted from the English papers first because I am sure they will amuse you.

"The great outline of the intended operations is "said to be this. If France does not absolutely relin-"quish her present treacherous conduct, which gives "her all the advantages of a war without any of the "dangers and losses — to declare war against her; "to send 50,000 foreign troops to America, which are "actually agreed for; to call home the frigates and "let them loose on the French commerce, and to form "a grand expedition with Gen¹ Howe's army against "the W. India Islands; to cede Gibralter and a sugar "island to Russia, on condition of the Empress send-"ing 40,000 men to North America. What seems to "confirm these circumstances is a commission going "to Holland to engage transports.

[The above appear'd in the London papers, a few days before the court of France had order'd the rebel vessels out of their ports, and prohibited the sale of their prizes.]

PHILADELPHIA.

"Last Thursday afternoon the rebels at Red-bank, horribly panick struck with the loss of their fort at Mud Island, which they looked upon as inaccessible and indeed was amazingly strong — blew up their magazine and fled from their fortifications which they had been preparing for these six or seven weeks past, with all the speed they were masters of, depending intirely on the nimbleness of their heels for their safety, and were heard by many of the citizens who were on the wharves looking at the vessels on fire, to cry with the greatest vociferation, 'Damn you — drive on — drive on — run my boys — the English are coming.'

"The same evening the brave commander of their fleet deserted by these their gallant comrades, set fire to two of their vessels, and sent them towards the city with the flood tide, but not having heart to put in execution their mischievous designs, quitted them before they reached the town — when they drifted on the Jersey shore and were burnt. Early the next morning with the first of the flood, they would fain have stolen by the city with the rest of the fleet, and for this purpose sent their galleys on first, which were so warmly saluted by the different batteries along shore and by the Delaware frigate, that it induced them rather to trust terra-firma than their floating fortresses for the security of their persons, and setting fire to their ships, kebecs, brigs, schooners, sloops, &ca., abandoned them — leaving their rigging, sails and every thing else on board, to the mercy of the flames, which burnt with such rapidity that it was impossible to save any part. Some of the vessels drove opposite to the town, where the fire reaching the guns which

were loaded, they went off, and shortly after their
magazines blew up with great explosions, but hap-
pily did no damage. In the conflagration, eight or
nine topsail vessels were consumed. Thus was a fleet
that cost the Congress and this province some hundred
thousand pounds, to their burning shame destroyed
in a few hours.

"It is with the greatest satisfaction the printer con-
gratulates his fellow citizens upon the happy fulfilment
of his hopes express'd in one of his former papers,
'that we sh^d shortly have the fleet lying before this
city'—and upon the happy renewal of business.
Nothing can afford every well-wisher to the prosperity
of this province greater joy than the present pleasing
view of our wharfs crowded with vessels and merchandise of every kind.

"Saturday morning last about 7 o'clock a pretty
smart shock of an earthquake was felt in this city.
It is about 14 years since any thing of an earthquake
has been felt here before.

"Whereas, notwithstanding the general agreement
of the inhabitants of this city — 'That such legal paper
money as has been emitted by acts of assembly, and
received the royal sanction, should be received in all
payments, and deemed of equal value with gold and
silver at the old customary rates, in the said agreement specified — sundry persons lately arrived in this
city, and even some who have signed the said agreement, do now refuse to take the said paper money

and make a difference in the prices if they can be paid
in gold and silver — thereby taking an injust advantage of the necessity of the times, striving to embarrass
the public affairs, to destroy the chief medium of
our commerce and prevent the negotiating bills of
exchange. We therefore to discourage practices so
selfish and injurious to the public, do hereby engage to
each other and the public upon our honor that we
will not directly or indirectly deal with any person or
persons whatsoever who shall refuse to take the said
paper money in their payments, or make any difference
between the value thereof and gold and silver as fixed
in the said agreement — nor will we deal with any
person or persons who shall be known to engross any
quantity of provisions, with a view to retail the same
at an immoderate price to the distress of the poor and
industrious housekeepers. The above association is
now signing by the Inhabitants at the Coffee House.' "

We have just received intelligence from Gen[l]
Greene and the Marquis de la Fayette that Morgan's
Corps with two pickets of militia, under the command
of the Marquis de la Fayette attacked the Hessian
Picket consisting of 300 men, kill'd 20, wounded about
as many and took 14 prisoners — the picket was twice
reinforced by British — night came on, and the Americans masters of the field march'd slowly to their
camp, having lost only two men kill'd and three or four
wounded.

I have barely time to close with those expressions of duty and affection which it always gives me pleasure to repeat.

JOHN LAURENS.

27th Novem., 1777.

The Honble Henry Laurens, Esqr.,
    President of Congress.

HEAD QUARTERS, 29th Novem., 1777.

My Dear Father :

I have just received and hastily read over your kind letter of the 27th and could write a great deal in answer to it if time or discretion would permit. This will merely serve as a cover to a newspaper, part of which I copied in my last. It goes by a man who is to set off immediately for York as I am informed by Col. Tilghman. I am exceedingly obliged to you for the gloves, and am ever

Your affectionate

JOHN LAURENS.

I must detain the messenger, who ever he be, while I relate an anecdote, which will give you some idea of the general misbehaviour of our navy.

When their retreat up the river was expected, the Delaware frigate was given over for lost — her guns were taken out, and only a few men left in her who were to make their escape immediately upon an attack from our fleet which was looked upon as an event that would certainly happen and that could not be otherwise than successful on our side.

If it were the custom for generals to proclaim their intentions, we had a right to expect an attack to-day; however, it is not amiss to be prepared for it. Gen¹ Greene has joined us, and our forces are reunited. The enemy after razing Bilingsport and Red Bank have quitted the Jerseys altogether. It appears that two British captains were kill'd and two wounded in the Marquis de la Fayette's combat.

Upon looking into your letter again I see that I am indebted to a lady for the gloves; you will oblige me by saying something handsome for me. My letter alluded to, began in the manner which you describe; it was a kind of journal which I had begun, and laid by in order to add to it occasionally.

The Honble Henry Laurens, Esq⟨r⟩.,
    President of Congress, York.

HEAD QUARTERS, 3ᵈ *December*, 1777.
My Dear Father:

I thank you for your kind letter of the 30ᵗʰ of last month, and the American Code of Public Law. I have given this book not such a reading as I wished, but such as my time permitted, and think it contains all the fundamental laws of a federative republic.

It is the part of the wise legislative body to make
12

the union of the states perpetual by procuring it the sanction of popular opinion.

If the majority of the people in each state, or only the majority of the states, can be persuaded that it is a religious duty, as was the case of the Greeks with respect to the Amphictionic League, or a duty to themselves as most favouring their private and political interests to maintain the confederation, it will be established upon the most permanent basis that human affairs admit of, and the opinion propagated by education will pass to remote posterity. I shall study these laws with the greatest attention in my retirement.

We have received several accounts from outposts within a few days past intimating that an attack upon us was meditated. We have in consequence prepared ourselves, paraded our men so as to make them acquainted with their ground and its advantages; but the enemy have remained within their works. Many are of opinion that Sr Wm Howe will not suffer any thing but mere necessity, or a very tempting prospect of decisive success, to call him from good winter quarters. Others say that from past experience he knows the vicinity of the Continental army to be exceedingly troublesome, and that it is his interest to drive us to a more respectable distance. In the mean time the season advances in which armies in general are forced to repair to more substantial shelter than tents, and whose inclemency is more particularly

grievous to our ill-clothed soldiers. The question is
whether we are to go into remote winter quarters,
and form a chain of cantonments in the interior part
of the country; leaving a vast extent of territory exposed to the devastation of an enraged unsparing
enemy; leaving inhabitants who will be partly seduced
by the expectation of gold, or more generally compell'd
to fill the traitorous provincial corps now raising;
leaving plentiful granaries and large stocks of cattle,
ample means for subsisting the troops and Tory citizens in Philadelphia, and for victualling transports
that may carry home Mr Burgoyne and his army;
leaving the well affected to fall a sacrifice, and deplore
our abandonment of them and the country; or,
whether we shall take a position more honourable, more
military, more republican, more consonant to the
popular wish — in a proper situation for covering the
country, or at least so much of it as circumstances will
permit — and for distressing and annoying the Enemy?

Winter campaigns it is said are ominous to the best
appointed and best disciplined armies. The misery
incident to them occasions desertion and sickness
which waste their numbers. Our army in particular
requires exemption from fatigue in order to compensate for their want of clothing.

Relaxation from the duties of a campaign, in order
to allow them an opportunity of being disciplined and
instructed; warm quarters, that it may appear in the
spring with undiminished numbers and in the full

prowess of health, &ca. Besides it is urged that the hardships which our soldiers undergo discourage men from enlisting. The answers that might be given in our particular circumstances to these general objections against winter campaigns are only for your private ear, and not to be trusted in a letter to the possibility of miscarriage; besides, we may take a position which will not absolutely expose us to a winter campaign, but furnish us excellent quarters for men at the same time that it leaves us within distance for taking considerable advantages of the enemy, and cover a valuable and extensive country.

As I hear that the Chevalier Failly intends for York, and it seems to be a matter of doubt whether any dispatches will go from head quarters to-day, I'll finish my letter and send it by him.

Gen¹ Dickinson made a descent some days ago on Staten Island which, if he had not been betrayed, would have thrown into his hands some very valuable prisoners and a large number of common ones. As it was, he took 2 lieutenants and 25 privates; made a secure retreat, and lost only two or three kill'd and wounded.

The triumviral committee from Congress arrived this evening. As much as I desire to see you, my dear father, I fear an interview cannot be effected for some time to come. Col. Hamilton who was sent to the Northern army to explain the necessity for reinforcements from thence, lies dangerously ill on the road. Since the battle of German Town, I have no longer been a supernumerary.

My heart is ever with you,

Your affectionate

JOHN LAURENS.

The Honble Henry Laurens Esqr.,

President of Congress, York.

Fav^d by M^r Le Chevalier De Failly.

HEAD QUARTERS, at the Gulf,

15th *December* 1777.

My Dear Father:

I have barely time to thank you for your packet of the 12th, and to express my great concern at the cause of your confinement. The pain arising from your malady must be aggravated by its happening at a time when you have the most important public affairs on your mind; but I hope it will neither be so durable nor so grievous as you seem to expect. Your own philosophy and the assurance of the sympathy of your friends will greatly mitigate the evil. I return two of the letters which you sent me, for your perusal; the others were from Mrs Laurens; the last dated gives me a title to expect her arrival in Carolina in company with Mr Blake's family.

The army cross'd the Schuylkil on the 13th and has remained encamped on the heights on this side. Our truly republican general has declared to his officers that he will set the example of passing the winter in a hut himself. The precise position is not as yet fixed upon, in which our huts are to be constructed; it will probably be determined this day; it must be in such a situation as to admit of a bridge of communication over the Schuylkil for the protection of the country we have just left; far enough from the enemy not to be reached in a day's march, and properly interposed between the enemy and the most valuable part of this country on this side Schuylkil.

With anxious prayers for your recovery,

I am your most dutiful and affectionate

JOHN LAURENS.

Berry received a hunting shirt and a check shirt. If there be any difficulty in getting him winter clothes I believe he can do without.

The last plundering and foraging party of the enemy under L⁴ Cornwallis on this side Schuylkil have gone beyond themselves in barbarous treatment of the inhabitants.

The Honble Henry Laurens,

President of Congress, York.

HEAD QUARTERS, 23ᵈ *December* 1777.

My Dear Father:

I wish it were in my power to enter properly into the different subjects which compose your letter of the 20ᵗʰ. In my present circumstances I must content myself with writing you a short and hasty epistle.

The particulars of the affair alluded to by the Chevalier de Failly, I took it for granted you would have received in your official letter, and therefore regretted the less my want of time to inform you properly of it. The matter was in brief as follows: when we march'd from Whitemarsh Camp, and were in the act of crossing the Schuylkil, we received intelligence that the enemy were advancing on this side of the river; in fact a ravaging party of four thousand under the command of Lord Cornwallis had pass'd the river and were driving Potter's Militia before them. Two regiments of this corps, however, are said to have conducted themselves extremely well and to have given the enemy no small annoyance as they advanced. General Sullivan was Major Gen¹ of the day and consequently conducted the march.

His division and part of Wayne's had cross'd the river; being uncertain as to the number of the enemy, and dreading their advance in force. When part of the army should be on one side of the river and part on the other he order'd those troops to recross and our bridge to be render'd impassible.

Notice of this was sent to the Commander in Chief, and when he arrived parties of the enemy were seen on the commanding heights on this side of the river. There was a pause for some time and consultation what was to be done; parties of horse in the mean time were detached to gain certain intelligence of the enemy's number and designs.

It was considered that our army was near a river to which it had march'd by a narrow road, on each side of which thick woods render'd it impossible for the army to display itself; and that if Sr Wm Howe sh^d keep up a show on the opposite side Schuylkil, and at the same time march in force from Philadelphia upon us, we must in these circumstances inevitably be ruined. Some pronounced hastily that the enemy had received intelligence of our march, although the resolution had been taken in council only the night before, and that they were prepared to oppose our passage. Genl Washington who never since I have been in his family has pass'd a false judgment on such points, gave it as his opinion that the party in view were foragers; that the meeting was accidental, but, however, the enemy might avail themselves of this unexpected discovery, and might draw as much advantage from it as if the rencounter had been premeditated.

The intelligence was received that the enemy were retiring in great haste, but it did not appear satisfactory, and the army was ordered to march to the Swedes Ford three or four miles higher up the river and encamp with the right to the Schuylkil. The next morning the want of provisions — I could weep tears of blood when I say it — the want of provisions render'd it impossible to march. We did not march till the evening of that day. Our ancient bridge, an infamous construction which in many parts obliged the men to march by Indian file, was restored, and a bridge of waggons made over the Swedes Ford, but fence-rails from necessity being substituted to plank, and furnishing a very unstable footing, this last served to cross a trifling number of troops. As the event turn'd out Gen¹ Sullivan's retrograde movement was unspeakably unlucky. If we had persevered in crossing in the first instance, or if we had even crossed in the evening of the first day, the flower of the British army must have fallen a sacrifice to superior numbers.

Among the parties of horse that were out upon this occasion a small detachment of Bland's Regiment composed of trumpeter, farrier, and whatever could be collected for the moment, their Col. at their head, charged a serjeant and guard of Hessians and took them all prisoners.

On the 19ᵗʰ inst. we march'd from the Gulph to this camp, head quarters at the Valley forge.

On the 22ⁿᵈ at night we received intelligence of a large foraging party of the enemy having pass'd the Schuylkil. Last evening the 22ᵈ Gen¹ Potter wrote us that General Howe is with the foragers, from whence we conclude that the greatest part of his army is with him. They encamped on the other side of Derby last night — will you believe it — starving in a plentiful country. The utmost we could do was to dispatch small parties draughted from each brigade last night, and to take extraordinary means for furnishing the army with provisions to enable a more respectable force to march to the enemy. Lᵈ Stirling's Division

13

march'd to-day in order to cover the country and observe the enemy's motions till something more effectual can be done.

I have inquired whence this defect in the Commissariat Department arises; but this must be defer'd till I next have the pleasure of writing to you. I have barely time to repeat my prayers for your speedy recovery, and the assurances of the boundless love of your

JOHN LAURENS.

Enclosed are letters of thanks, one in French and an attempt at one in English, by way of translation, from Lt Col. Fleury. By the bye my military title is Lt Colonel.

The Honble Henry Laurens, Esqr.,
     President of Congress, York.

HEAD QUARTERS, 1st *Jan.*, 1778.

My Dear Father:

I am much disappointed in being obliged to write you a short and hasty letter, and sorry to send you only the translation of one of your French pieces. Col. Barton, who brought me your letter of the 25th, made me happy by informing me that you were in a fair way of recovery; in that of the 23^d that you had recourse to your old experiment of cold water. Genl Mc Intosh had told me that you were trying the effects of this uncommon application, and it made me uneasy; but I cannot help applauding it as it has succeeded.

Inclosed is a letter from Holland, and one from Mrs Manning, to which the former served as cover. The blunder of our friend is unaccountable, but I am in hopes it will not be attended with the pernicious consequence which you seem to apprehend, as it will not be easy to ascertain or take hold of the property which you may have in private hands against the will of the party holding it. Capt Nichols is not yet returned from Philadelphia; I have sent a message to him by the deputy Com^y of prisoners who went in to-day, and I have no doubt that the Capt will wait upon you if he comes out again.

Genl Smallwood who commands a division posted at Wilmington, has given us information that upon hearing of an armed brig being aground five miles above his post, he detached a strong party with two field pieces to take her. The Capt of the brig upon the first summons refused to surrender, thinking the party was armed only with musquetry and prepared for defending himself; but being undeceived by two or three cannon shot, he struck. The prisoners taken on board of her are a British captain of foot, 67 privates, the master of the brig, 12 seamen and about 40 women, some of whom are officers' wives. The cargo is said to consist of clothing for soldiers, some arms and ammunition, some liquors, officers' baggage and camp equipage; however, we do not know exactly. The captain of foot was too sulky to be communicative, and the master says the contents of the bales are unknown to him. The brig is armed with six four pounders and a few swivels. A sloop laden with pork, flour, &ca., for the Philadelphia market is likewise taken and will be either burnt or secured as circumstances will permit.

The enemy returned to Philadelphia last Sunday after having completed their forage, without any other inconvenience than a small balance of prisoners against them. It seems they had been necessitated to come out by having imprudently packed their former plunder of hay before it was thoroughly dry, by which means the greatest part was damaged and they were reduced to four days' allowance in this article.

The soldiers are nearly covered with good huts. The North Carolinians are the most backward in their buildings, and for want of sufficient energy to exert themselves once for all, will be exposed to lasting evils.

The promotion of Gen¹ Conway has given almost universal disgust. His military knowledge and experience may fit him for the office of inspector general, but the right of seniority violated, without any remarkable services done to justify it, has given a deep wound to the line of brigadiers.

It is said that the influence of a certain general officer at Reading is productive of great mischief. When Gen¹ Conway went from camp he gave out that he meant to return to France, his countrymen understood the manœuvre: it has succeeded to his wish, and I believe now he is exceedingly indifferent whether he acts Insp^r Genl or no. I am rather inclined to think that he prefers returning with his splendid titles to France, where he hopes to obtain a lucrative and peaceful office in the service of the states.

I devoutly pray that many new years of happiness may be added to your life.

Your most affectionate
JOHN LAURENS.

The Chevalier du Plessis who commanded the artillery and acted as engineer at Fort Mercer has obtained a promise from his Excellency, to write in his behalf to Congress in order that his merit may be rewarded by promotion — as from the improvements which he made at Fort Mercer and his gallant conduct when Count Donop was repulsed, he deserves well of the United States; if the general should recommend him in consequence of his promise, which I suppose he will do whenever his time permits, I would solicit that the reasons for the Chevalier's promotion may be express'd in the resolve of Congress, which will be of great service to him in France.

The Honble Henry Laurens, Esqr,

l'resident of Congress, York.

HEAD QUARTERS, 3^d Jan., 1778.

My Dear Father:

By this day's courier, you will be informed of a base insult offer'd to the Commander in chief, which will raise your indignation.

A preliminary anecdote may throw some light upon this matter. Some time ago, his Exc⁷ received a letter from a friend, enclosing a piece of paper with the following words : "In a letter to Gen¹ Gates, Gen¹ Conway says, ' Heaven has been determined to save your country, or a weak general and bad counsellors would have ruined it.' The gen¹ immediately copied the contents of the paper, introducing them with *sir*, and concluding with, ' I am your humble serv',' and sent this copy in form of a letter to Gen¹ Conway." This drew an answer, in which he first attempts to deny the fact, and then in a most shameless manner, to explain away the word *weakness*. The perplexity of his style, and evident insincerity of his compliments, betray his real sentiments, and expose his guilt.

After this, he certainly had no right to expect cordiality on the part of the general, but he has always been treated with that kind of civility, which resulted from a consideration of his public character, abstracted from his private one. He experienced that kind of complaisance, which passes current in the transactions of men, and in which the heart is not concerned. Indeed you will think, perhaps, the General's delicacy on this point led him to too great forbearance when you learn that Gen¹ Conway was charged with cowardice at the battle of German Town, and that a gentleman of rank and reputation, desir'd to be called upon as an evidence. It is notorious that he disobey'd his orders, and that he was for a considerable time separated from his brigade. The Gen¹, however, thinking that a public investigation of this matter set on foot by him, might be attribut'd to motives of personal resentment, suffer'd it to pass over. When Gen¹ C. left camp, pretending that he was determined to return to France, his countrymen discerned his real intentions, and gave him credit for the manœuvre.

He has weight it seems with a certain party, formed against the present Commander in chief, at the head of which is Gen¹ Mifflin. His own preposterous panegyricks of himself, and the influence of this junto, have probably gained him the extraordinary promotion, which has convulsed the army. His reception at camp was consonant to the Genl's uniform conduct towards him, since the epoch above alluded to; the complaisance due to his rank was exercised towards him.

What has passed since, you will be properly informed of. His last letter, which is a most insolent attempt at what the French call *persiflage*, or humouring a man, affects the Gen¹ very sensibly.

It is such an affront as Conway would never have dared to offer, if the General's situation had not assured him of the impossibility of its being revenged in a private way. The Gen¹, therefore, has determined to return him no answer at all, but to lay the whole matter before Congress; they will determine whether Gen¹ W. is to be sacrificed to Gen¹ C., for the former can never consent to be concern'd in any transaction with the latter, from whom he has received such unpardonable insults. My private opinion is, that Conway never meant to act as Inspector Gen[l], or to carry his new grade of major general into the field; but that his vanity being amply gratified by his exaltation, not only above the brigadiers, but even the major generals, he was desirous of retiring to a more lucrative and less dangerous employment in the service of the states at home. I hope that some virtuous and patriotic men, will form a countermine to blow up the pernicious junto spoken of above.

I have taken the liberty of writing to you my dear father on this subject, in order that you might be more minutely acquainted with it.

I have been obliged to do it in a hurry, and in a small, noisy, crowded room. I have succeeded so far with secrecy, and dare not venture upon a more decent copy. I hope, therefore, that you will excuse my letter, and accept it in its present dress.

I hope it will find you perfectly reliev'd from your old enemy, the gout, and in condition to save America from her most dangerous enemies.

Your most affectionate
JOHN LAURENS.

I hope Congress will not lose sight of the office of inspector gen[l].

The Honble Henry Laurens, Esq[r],

    President of Congress.

HEAD QUARTERS, *5th Jan.*, 1778.

My Dear Father:

Some commercial technicalities puzzled me in the letters which you sent me to translate. My French acquaintance here are almost as much at a loss how to render the words in question, as much as I was myself; however, I believe the following explanations are right: *fonsage*, one of the articles of charge in the account sales, signifies, *filling up, or packing;* it stands thus in the original, *au tonnelier pour fonsage & foncage*, i. e., *to the cooper for packing gabarage;* another charge is properly cooperage, or repairs to the cask.

Livraison, another charge, means the *delivery;* but I can't explain what delivery is to be understood, as it is unconnected with any other word.

Babut & Labouchere in one of their letters say, " We are sorry the goods per Capt Cochran were *avariés.* The blank in this part of my translation is to be supplied with the word *averaged;* the cargo, I suppose, received some damage at sea.

In another letter, where they relate the prices curr^t, *goudron* means *tar*, and *bray*, I can only guess, means *green tar*, for it is placed among the productions of the pine tree, and it cannot signify pitch, for that is express'd by *poix.* I am exceedingly sorry that my ignorance in these matters has made me bungle so, but hope there will be no ill consequence arise from it.

The continuance of your pains is a great affliction

14

to me; and if sympathy can alleviate, or prayers avail
to remove the evil, the tenderness of the former causes
the latter incessantly to flow from

> Your affectionate
> JOHN LAURENS.

Inclosed is a newspaper, which, though not of a very
recent date, may afford you some amusement. The
means which are taken in Philadelphia to discredit the
report of a French war, are to me, better proof in our
favor, than many testimonies that are exhibited on
our part.

The Honble Henry Laurens, Esq[r].,
> President of Congress, York.

> HEAD QUARTERS, 14*th Jan.*, 1778.

My Dear Father:

This will be delivered to you by the Chevalier de
Mauduit de Plessis, whose name I mentioned to you
in one of my late letters. I am happy in having an
opportunity of recommending so worthy a man to your
protection. He was employed by the Commander in
chief, to act at Red Bank in the capacities of engineer
and commandant of artillery, and acquitted himself
so well as to obtain panegyricks approaching to rap-
ture from the officers who were witnesses of his conduct. The alterations which he made in the works of
his post shew'd that he had not confined himself to

one branch of military knowledge, but had extended . his studies with success to one which is generally held as a mystery apart. His admirable behaviour during the action which proved fatal to so many daring Hessians; his saving some valuable artillery and stores by preferring the public interest to his own safety; his exposing his life by blowing up the magazine at Fort Mercer without the preparation which is usually made in such cases for the security of the operator, and his gallant conduct on all occasions, entitle him to the promotion which his Excellency solicits for him. The letter which Mr. Duplessis now carries to Congress would have gone in the order of time, if his modesty had not made him backward in speaking of himself. I interest myself greatly in his success because I know his merit. As this is the only reason that can prevail with you to befriend any man who is soliciting public reward, I recommend this gentleman with confidence; and if it is in your power to assist him in procuring a brevet of lieutenant colonel, expressing the reasons for his promotion, and bearing date the 26th November, in order that those who are not his seniors in France may not have a right to command him here, I entreat you to do it, as you will essentially serve a young man, whose military ardour and talents make him valuable to the United States.

I am with every sentiment of filial affection your

JOHN LAURENS.

As there is a great demand for commissions, his

Excellency desires me to apply for a large number of blanks to be sent by the next courier.

The Honble Henry Laurens, Esqr.,

President of Congress.

HEAD QUARTERS, 14*th* *Jan.*, 1778.

I barely hinted to you, my dearest father, my desire to augment the Continental forces from an untried source. I wish I had any foundation to ask for an extraordinary addition to those favours which I have already received from you. . I would solicit you to cede me a number of your able bodied men slaves, instead of leaving me a fortune.

I would bring about a two-fold good ; first, I would advance those who are unjustly deprived of the rights of mankind to a state which would be a proper gradation between abject slavery and perfect liberty, and besides I would reinforce the defenders of liberty with a number of gallant soldiers. Men, who have the habit of subordination almost indelibly impressed on them, would have one very essential qualification of soldiers. I am persuaded that if I could obtain authority for the purpose, I would have a corps of such men trained, uniformly clad, equip'd and ready in every respect to act at the opening of the next campaign. The ridicule that may be thrown on the color, I despise, because I am sure of rendering essential service to my country. I am tired of the languor with which so sacred a war as this is carried on. My circumstances prevent me from writing so long a letter as I expected and wish'd to have done on a subject which I have much at heart. I entreat you to give a favorable answer to

Your most affectionate
JOHN LAURENS.

The Honble Henry Laurens, Esqr.,
   President of Congress.

HEAD QUARTERS, 23d Jan., 1778.

My Dear Father:

I wish it were in my power to enter fully into every part of your kind letters dated the 8th and 16th inst., but as that will be impossible by the present opportunity I must confine myself to thanking you for the information which you have given me in some important points, and replying briefly to several questions which you ask me:

First, the Baron d' Arendt is a German, who served as he says in quality of aide de camp to the K. of Prussia; was colonel in our service of a battalion of Germans and their descendants raised in Maryland and this State, was sent afterwards to take the command at Fort Mifflin where his ill health suffered him to stay but a short time. He has undoubtedly great military talents; but I have heard that Genl Muhlenberg, who commanded the brigade to which the German regiment is attached, and the officers of the regiment, call the baron's probity into question. His Excellency has neither seen nor heard any thing of this gentleman that could give him an unfavourable opinion of him.

We have never had any particular account of the prizes in the Delaware. One or two of those taken on the Jersey shore, from their vicinity to Philadelphia yielded but little profit to the captors, as they were obliged to burn them before they could unload them.

The Chevalier de Neuville with his brother and companions sets out for York to-morrow. I take the Cheval^r to be a gentleman whose thirst for glory, and whose military knowledge would make him an acquisition to the army of the United States. The younger brother as far as I can judge from his appearance, tho' inferior in knowledge, is animated with sentiments that characterize the soldier.

The resolution of Congress respecting Genl Burgoyne and his army, I think both founded in justice and policy. It might have been better perhaps if a little more republican laconism had been used in explaining the reasons for it.

The letter said to be the general's is partly genuine and partly spurious. Those who metamorphosed the intercepted original committed an error in point of time, for Mrs. Washington was with the general in New York at the date of it.

You asked me, my dear father, what bounds I have

set to my desire of serving my country in the military line ? I answer glorious death, or the triumph of the cause in which we are engaged.

I must not conclude without giving you a short account of a brilliant defence lately made by a few of Capt Lee's troop. Near two hundred of the enemy's light dragoons made an attempt to surprise the captain in his quarters. They concealed their march by a circuitous road, and arrived at the house a little after day-break conducted by an intelligent guide. Lee had at the time with him only his lieutenant, Mr. Lindsay, a corporal and four privates, and Major Jameson of the same regiment who happen'd to be there on a visit. They posted themselves in the house and made the necessary preparations for defence. Capt. Delancy, who commanded the enemy's advanced guard, led it on bravely 'till he arrived under cover of the eves, while the main body kept up a constant fire from a distance on the windows. After repeated efforts had been made to enter the house, the party repulsed made an attempt to seize the horses which were in the stable, but such a well directed constant fire was kept up from the house that the bravest dragoon did not venture to dismount. The loss of the enemy was one commissioned officer and three or four privates. The party in its retreat picked up a quarter-master's serjeant and a couple of videttes. Lieutenant Lindsay was wounded in the hand. Too much praise cannot be bestowed upon the officers and men who had the honor of forcing such an incomparable superiority of numbers to a shameful retreat. Capt Nichols was at Lee's quarters in his way from Philadelphia during the action, and gives our little party great applause as I have been told.

We have some as brave individuals among our officers as any that exist. Our men are the best crude materials for soldiers I believe in the world, for they possess a docility and patience which astonish foreigners. With a little more discipline we should drive the haughty Briton to his ships.

I am unhappy in hearing that your leg continues so weak, and wish that I could offer my shoulder as a support; but at this distance, I can only help you by my prayers, and comfort by assurances of sympathy.

Your most affectionate

JOHN LAURENS.

The Honble Henry Laurens, Esqr.,

    President of Congress, York.

    (Private).

HEAD QUARTERS, 28th Jan., 1778.

My Dear Father:

The Marquis de Lafayette gives me an opportunity of thanking you for your kind letter of the 25th. The intended expedition to Canada that gentleman had communicated to me the day before in confidence, and by giving me the perusal of his letter to you on the subject had discovered his aversion to a certain general as second in command.

The policy of the enterprise does not appear to me good in our present circumstances, for altho' numbers may be employed in this that could not be engaged in any other, counting volunteers from the Eastern states and the well affected of the country into which the war is carried, yet a certain quantity of strength and treasure will be employed, which might be better applied elsewhere. I am speaking on the supposition that it is impossible for us to hold our conquests in Canada, while the enemy continues superior to us by sea.

Towns and fortifications and some military stores may be destroyed; the unhappy Canadians will be forced to side by turns with the party in possession, and experience the redoubled horrors of war.

The organization of the force which we are to use, as far as we are acquainted with it here, does not give satisfaction. It is feared that the ambition and intriguing spirit of Conway will be subversive of the public good, while he will proceed securely behind the shield of his commanding officer, taking to himself the merit of every thing praiseworthy and attributing every misfortune to the ostensible head. The person who is appointed Q. master for this expedition, is said to be a man skilfull in enriching himself at the public expense.

Our friend the Mˢ. knowing the existence of a certain faction, and penetrating the character of his

15

second, has prudently resolved to wait upon Congress, and to find out the extent of their views in sending forces into Canada, that he may act correspondently and not have the secret of their intentions deposited in another man while he has the command.

I cannot altogether clear up the matter which you allude to. I think I told you in my first letters on the subject whence the general derived his knowledge of the existence of the insolent paragraph, and it does not appear extraordinary to me that a certain gentleman who was capable of writing it, should afterwards deny it.

I am called upon to attend the general to his first official interview with the congressional committee, and have time only to repeat that I am ever,

Your

JOHN LAURENS.

The Honble Henry Laurens, Esq\r.,
President of Congress, York.

HEAD QUARTERS, 2*d Feb.*, 1778.

My Dear Father:

The more I reflect upon the difficulties and delays which are likely to attend the completing our Continental regiments, the more anxiously is my mind bent upon the scheme, which I lately communicated to you. The obstacles to the execution of it had presented themselves to me, but by no means appeared insur-

mountable. I was aware of having that monstrous
popular prejudice, open-mouthed against me, of under-
taking to transform beings almost irrational, into well
disciplined soldiers, of being obliged to combat the
arguments, and perhaps the intrigues, of interested
persons. But zeal for the public service, and an ardent
desire to assert the rights of humanity, determined me
to engage in this arduous business, with the sanction
of your consent. My own perseverance, aided by the
countenance of a few virtuous men, will, I hope,
enable me to accomplish it.

You seem to think, my dear father, that men recon-
ciled by long habit to the miseries of their condition,
would prefer their ignominious bonds to the untasted
sweets of liberty, especially when offer'd upon the
terms which I propose.

I confess, indeed, that the minds of this unhappy
species must be debased by a servitude, from which
they can hope for no relief but death, and that every
motive to action but fear, must be nearly extinguished
in them. But do you think they are so perfectly
moulded to their state as to be insensible that a better
exists? Will the galling comparison between themselves and their masters leave them unenlightened in
this respect? Can their self love be so totally annihi-
lated as not frequently to induce ardent wishes for a
change?

You will accuse me, perhaps, my dearest friend, of
consulting my own feelings too much; but I am

tempted to believe that this trampled people have so much human left in them, as to be capable of aspiring to the rights of men by noble exertions, if some friend to mankind would point the road, and give them a prospect of success. If I am mistaken in this, I would avail myself, even of their weakness, and, conquering one fear by another, produce equal good to the public. You will ask in this view, how do you consult the benefit of the slaves? I answer, that like other men, they are the creatures of habit. Their cowardly ideas will be gradually effaced, and they will be modified anew. Their being rescued from a state of perpetual humiliation, and being advanced, as it were, in the scale of being, will compensate the dangers incident to their new state.

The hope that will spring in each man's mind, respecting his own escape, will prevent his being miserable. Those who fall in battle will not lose much; those who survive will obtain their reward. Habits of subordination, patience under fatigues, sufferings and privations of every kind, are soldierly qualifications, which these men possess in an eminent degree.

Upon the whole, my dearest friend and father, I hope that my plan for serving my country and the oppressed negro race will not appear to you the chimera of a young mind, deceived by a false appearance of moral beauty, but a laudable sacrifice of private interest, to justice and the public good.

You say, that my resources would be small, on account of the proportion of women and children. I do not know whether I am right, for I speak from impulse, and have not reasoned upon the matter. I say, altho' my plan is at once to give freedom to the negroes, and gain soldiers to the states; in case of concurrence, I sh^d sacrifice the former interest, and therefore w^d change the women and children for able-bodied men. The more of these I could obtain, the better; but forty might be a good foundation to begin upon.

It is a pity that some such plan as I propose could not be more extensively executed by public authority. A well chosen body of 5,000 black men, properly offi-cer'd, to act as light troops, in addition to our present establishment, might give us decisive success in the next campaign.

I have long deplored the wretched state of these men, and considered in their history, the bloody wars excited in Africa, to furnish America with slaves — the groans of despairing multitudes, toiling for the luxuries of merciless tyrants.

I have had the pleasure of conversing with you, sometimes, upon the means of restoring them to their rights. When can it be better done, than when their enfranchisement may be made conducive to the pub-lic good, and be modified, as not to overpower their weak minds?

You ask, what is the general's opinion, upon this

subject? He is convinced, that the numerous tribes of blacks in the southern parts of the continent, offer a resource to us that should not be neglected. With respect to my particular plan, he only objects to it, with the arguments of pity for a man who would be less rich than he might be.

I am obliged, my dearest friend and father, to take my leave for the present; you will excuse whatever exceptionable may have escaped in the course of my letter, and accept the assurance of filial love, and respect of

Your

JOHN LAURENS.

HEAD QUARTERS, 3d Feb.

My Dear Father:

I am happy in having an opportunity of introducing to your acquaintance the brave Col° Fleury, whose reputation is not unknown to you. At the same time, I cannot but regret that he is called to another employment when I was in hopes of having engaged him as a colleague and coadjutor in raising the famous black battalion, with which I have troubled you so much lately.

The resolutions of Congress is a sufficient recommendation of this young gentleman to your notice. I will only add, that I am happy in having laid the foundation of what I hope will be an inviolable friendship with him.

> Your most dutiful and affectionate
> JOHN LAURENS.

The Honble Henry Laurens, Esqr.,
>   President of Congress.

> HEAD QUARTERS, 3*d* *Feb.*, 1778.

My Dear Father:

I am happy in having the pleasure of introducing to your acquaintance, Colonel Fitzgerald, the senior aid in our family.

His affairs call him to Virginia, and as he means to pass through York Town, you will have an opportunity of learning many things, *viva voce*, from him, which are not so well committed to writing.

> Your most dutiful and affectionate
> JOHN LAURENS.

> HEAD QUARTERS, 9*th* *Feb.*, 1778.

I have to thank you, my dear father, for two shirts, and a piece of scarlet cloth. I wrote to James for some hair powder and pomatum, but received only the latter with a comb. As I am upon the subject of dress, it will not be premature to inform you, that if you should command me to remain in my present station, blue and buff cloth, lining, twist, yellow flat double gilt buttons sufficient to make me a uniform suit, will be wanted; besides, corded dimity for waist-coats and breeches against the opening of the campaign; and I must beg the favour of you to write to some friend in South Carolina, to procure me these articles. A pair of gold epaulettes and a saddle cloth may be added, if not too expensive. If you should give me leave to execute my black project, my uniform will be a white field (faced with red), a color which is easiest kept clean, and will form a good contrast with the complexion of the soldier.

Inclosed are two letters from Duplessis, which relate to his commission. Upon his arrival here, he asked for a regimental commission, in addition to that which had been given him by Congress.

The general refused it, as he looked upon the resolve to have intended only a brevet, and that a regimental commission might produce a concurrence between him and senior artillery officers, which would be the occasion of discontent, and perhaps the resignation of some valuable men.

Duplessis understands it differently, and, hoping that he is in the right, applies to you.

You know my opinion of this gentleman's merit, but I must confess at the same time, that I think the brevet is a very honourable and handsome reward of his services.

It is said here, that Mr. Fleury is soliciting at York a farther promotion; I am exceedingly sorry to hear it.

All his countrymen agree that he is amply rewarded, and that as there was great analogy between the services render'd by him and Duplessis, no greater recompense should be accorded to one than to the other. If Fleury is made a colonel, Duplessis will have the right to ask the same rank, and so they may go on 'till they have exhausted all the rank that exists among us. It is a pity that Congress should grant any promotions but upon the recommendation of those superior officers, who have known or seen the feats upon which the pretensions are founded. The present way of proceeding is productive of great confusion and much uneasiness. It is complained, that whoever will go to York and speak loudly to members of Congress, of his own abilities and eminent services, will obtain what he intrigues for. One improper promotion induces another, and perhaps several others to silence the murmurers, and rank and Congress, I am sorry to say it, but I speak with the bleeding heart of a republican, they are both brought into contempt by it. The august representative body of thirteen free states is said to be bullied by every man who is impudent enough to make his own panegyrick, and represent his own importance.

I could not forbear communicating a part of your favour of 3ᵈ inst., to our friend; he seems sensible that the gentleman, who you mention to have conversed with you upon certain matters, is only the instrument of more dangerous and inveterate personages.

Mr. Payne has obligingly offer'd to take charge of my letter. I have just discovered that he is waiting for it, and as it grows dark and he has a bad road to travel, I must not farther trespass upon his good nature.

Your most affectionate
JOHN LAURENS.

The Honble Henry Laurens, Esq'.,
   President of Congress, York.

HEAD QUARTERS, 9th Feb., 1778.

My Dear Father:

I have just finished a few hasty lines and dispatched Mr. Payne, but in my hurry I forgot to inform you of an interesting letter which the general received this morning from Sir Wm. Howe, in which he declares that he is ready to give his consent to a general exchange of prisoners upon the terms formerly offered by Gen'. Washington, alledging his desire to relieve the men and officers from the misery which unavoid-ably accompanies captivity, as his only motive. He disavows the cruel treatment of our prisoners with which he has been so often charged; and quotes the license which he has lately given to our commissaries to purchase blanketing for the unhappy American captives, to establish his reputation in point of human-ity. He farther says he is informed that the claims upon Lieut. Gen' Burgoyne's army for provisions have been made a pretext for infringing if not totally breaking the convention of Saratoga, and says he will give orders for liquidating accounts of this nature and paying the balances, when he hopes the proper orders will be given by Gen. Washington for the embarcation of the convention troops. But as this letter is not announced to you officially, I must entreat you to let the existence of it remain a secret with yourself.

The Marquis de Lafayette left camp on Friday. Duplessis set out this morning. They both have told me things which humble me as a republican. Our freedom depends upon the patriotic exertions of a few individuals. It is with grief I learn that Congress is composed of so small a number as fifteen. The state of Virginia you see has assented to the articles of confederation. Is there not some latent eastern policy in the article which requires a majority of nine voices to four to decide every important general question? Adieu, my dear friend and father. I can not form a better wish for my country, than that it had more men like you. The paucity of such citizens is an unanswerable argument for your remaining in public office.

I am with the greatest respect and tenderest affection,

Your

JOHN LAURENS.

A day or two ago, a handsome young lad, who call'd himself Cope, and said he was an ensign in the 55th British. He said that in an affair of honor, he had killed his man, and fearing the consequences, threw himself into our protection. He was treated with that generosity which I hope will ever characterize Americans. A collection of clothes and money was made for him; the Marquis took him with him, and is to furnish him with letters for his friends in France. We have since discovered that he is an impostor. A duel has lately been fought in which an officer was killed, but Cope was not concerned in it. It is probable that he is some young officer who has been obliged to fly in consequence of some disgraceful action, or perhaps a series of follies. I just had time to send the Marquis a message by Duplessis to put him on his guard.

HEAD QUARTERS, 15*th Feb.*, 1778.

My Dear Father:

I am to thank you for your kind letter of the 6th inst., and the two camp shirts which accompanied it. The presumption which would lead me to pursue my project after what you have said upon it, would be unpardonable; praying your forgiveness therefor, my dear friend, for the trouble which I have given you on this eccentric scheme, I renounce it as a thing which cannot be sanctified by your approbation. At the same time, I must confess to you that I am very sensibly affected by your imputing my plan in so large a degree to ambition. I declare upon my honor that I would not have desired any other than my present rank, and that I would even have taken the title of captain of an independent corps, for the pleasure of serving my country so usefully, as I fondly hoped I should have been able to do, had my scheme been carried into execution.

The scarlet cloth, four camp shirts (in all), a roll of pomatum, a hair comb, two shirts for Berry, and a hunting shirt, have been received at different times, and I am exceedingly obliged to you for them. In future I will be more careful to thank you for such articles immediately after the receipt of them.

The express is waiting only for my letter, which circumstance has obliged me to write in haste, and force me to take leave. I am

Your most affectionate and dutiful

JOHN LAURENS.

The Honble Henry Laurens, Esqr.,
    President of Congress, York.

HEAD QUARTERS, 17th Feb., 1778.

My Dear Father:

I have to ask pardon for omitting to inform you what was done with the letter for Mr. Bringhurst. The day after its arrival here, Mr. Chaloner, one of our commissaries, set out for German Town, on some business, and took charge of it. As he has not since returned to camp, I am not yet acquainted of the fate of it.

We have lately been in a most alarming situation for want of provisions. The soldiers were scarcely restrained from mutiny by the eloquence and management of our officers. Those who are employed to feed us, either for want of knowledge or for want of activity or both, never furnish supplies adequate to our wants.

I have more than once mentioned to you that we have been obliged to renounce the most important enterprises, delay the most critical marches, by the delinquency of commissaries. Here of late it has reduced us almost to the point of disbanding. The head of the department is a stationary attendant on Congress; what he might do if he had views sufficiently extensive, by a proper employment of agents, I know not; but as the case is at present, he seems to be almost useless. I have heard it asserted by more than one sensible, disinterested man, that the removal of Mr. Trumbull from that office has been the source of all our misfortunes. He had considerable connections and influence in a great meat country, and had laid such a train for supplying the army, as in all probability would have put us out of the reach of bad weather, difficult roads and other common accidents. Certain it is that the want of providence, or want of ability in the present managers, has brought us to the brink of ruin. By extraordinary exertions, by scraping from distant scanty magazines and collecting with parties, we have obtained a temporary relief; and have hopes that the representation of our late distress to several persons of influence and authority in different states, will procure us such farther supplies as will save us from the disagreeable necessity of dividing the army into cantonments.

To the ill offices of Trumbull's friends we may attribute perhaps a part of our distress. The increasing number of privateers in the New England states, the subsistence of the convention troops, and an expedition now on foot, will greatly diminish the meat resources of the country on which we principally depend. The carcasses of horses about the camp, and the deplorable leanness of those which still crawl in existence, speak the want of forage equal to that of human food. General Greene with a party of two thousand, is now foraging, but will be able to collect only the gleanings of a country over which an unsparing enemy has passed.

A small detachment from his party under the command of Major Bullard, made an attempt to surprise the enemy's picket near their bridge. The design was discovered and the picket had time to post itself in a stone house, at the distance of 500 yards. Our men were saluted with a general discharge; they marched forward and returned the fire, and would have proceeded to storming the house, but it was thought more advisable to retire. Our party had five men slightly wounded; the enemy's loss was one Hessian killed, and another mortally wounded.

Gen¹. Wayne is detached by Gen¹ Greene to cross the Delaware at Wilmington, for the purpose of destroying all the hay on the Jersey shore which we cannot secure for our own use, and which may fall into the enemy's hands, and with a view of driving all the cattle from the neighborhood of the river, by a circuitous road to camp. If he finds it practicable to cross the river and carry that plan into execution, he is to make a large sweep and return here with whatever he can collect by the way of Gorshen.

The disaffected inhabitants find means to conceal their teams and cattle, so that the country appears more naked than it really is.

Deserters from the enemy inform us that they are preparing for a grand forage, and that they will probably make it in Bucks county. We have the same business in contemplation in the same place.

I must not omit informing you of a gallant defence made by a justice of the peace in Philadelphia county (on the other side of the Schuylkil), known by the appellation of Squire Knox. This gentleman's house was surrounded early in the morning some days ago by a party of traitors, lately distinguished by the title of royal refugees; he was in bed in a lower room, and upon their demanding admittance, was going to open

to them, when his son who was above, and perceiving
from the window fixed bayonets, call'd to him to keep
his door shut and warned him of danger. The villains in the mean time pressed against the door;
the old man armed himself with his cutlass, and his
son descended with a gun. The door was at length
forced half open by one of the most enterprising;
the father kept it in that position with his left hand,
and employed his right in defending the passage.
After some vigorous strokes, his cutlass broke; the
bad condition of the son's fusil had prevented his
firing till this moment. He was now prepared to salute
the assailants, but the old man thinking all was lost by
the failure of his weapon, called to him not to fire;
upon farther examination, however, he says he found
that by being shortened, it was only better adapted
to close quarters, and renewed the fight.

The villains fired seven shots through the door, one
of which grazed the squire's knee, which was all the
damage done. They then threw down their arms and
took to their heels; they were pursued by the Knoxes
and a family of militia, and one of them who was
concealed in a cellar was taken.

The besetting Mr. Knox's house is a matter of civil
cognizance, but it appears that the prisoner has held
correspondence with the enemy, and supplied them
with provisions, and he will probably suffer death for
those offences by sentence of court-martial.

It is said that a number of deserters from the
17

convention troops have found means to introduce themselves as substitutes among the militia.

Don't you think my dear father that this matter should be provided against? I have insensibly written a letter, which perhaps you will not have time to read. It is not uncommon, however, to look at the exordium and peroration; you may think it policy therefore in me to repeat my request for cloths in this place, but I assure you it was accidental. You will by complying with it contribute to the propriety of the Commander in chief's family, and infinitely oblige,

Your most affectionate

JOHN LAURENS.

The Honble Henry Laurens, Esqr.,

 Favd by Colonel Harvey.

My Dear Father:

I have barely time to thank you for your kind favour of the eighteenth, and the pleasure of Baron Steuben's acquaintance. Nothing that depends on me shall be wanting to make his stay in camp agreeable, and if he enters into service, to make myself useful to him. I deplore the misfortune of Charlestown if it has fallen upon individuals of moderate fortune; if it affects only a number of rich men, it will contribute to equalizing estates, I shall not regret it.

Garçon being masculine, requires the article to be

of the same gender; therefore, *une*, which is feminine, makes a false concord; take away the *e* final and make it *un*, all will be right.

I am, my dear father, ever your affectionate and dutiful

JOHN LAURENS.

———

HEAD QUARTERS, 24*th Feb.*, 1778.

I have but one pair of breeches that are wearable. If James can possibly procure me some white cloth to reinforce me in this article, it will be of great service to me.

The Honble Henry Laurens, Esqr.,

President of Congress, York.

———

HEAD QUARTERS, 28*th Feb.*, 1778.

My Dear Father:

I was obliged to write briefly and in haste, by the last courier. I have since had several long conversations with the Baron Steuben, who appears to me a man profound in the science of war, and well disposed to render his best services to the United States. In an interview between him and the general, at which I assisted in quality of interpreter, he declared that he had purposely waved making any contract with Congress, previous to his having made some acquaintance with the Commander in chief, in order that he might avoid giving offence to the officers of the army, and that the general might decide, in what post he could be the most useful. If I have conceived rightly of his character and abilities, he would make us an excellent quarter master general, in the military part of the department; his office being confined to the choice of positions, regulation of marches, etc. But as the civil and military duties with us are blended, he can't be disposed of in this way; his being a foreigner, unfitting him totally for the latter. I think he would be the properest man we could choose for the office of inspector general, and there are several good assistants that might be given him. I have the highest opinion of the service he would render in this line, as he seems to be perfectly aware of the disadvantages under which our army has labored from short enlistments and frequent changes; seems to understand what our soldiers are capable of, and is not so staunch a systematist as to be averse from adapting established forms to stubborn circumstances. He will not give us the perfect instructions, absolutely speaking, but the best which we are in a condition to receive. We want some kind of general tutoring in this way so much, that as obnoxious as Conway is to most of the army, rather than take the field without the advantages that might be derived from a judicious exercise of his office, I would wish every motive of dissatisfaction respecting him for the present to be suppressed.

The baron proposes to take the rank of major general, with the pay, rations, etc. He does not wish for any actual command, as he is not acquainted with our language and the genius of our people.

It gives great uneasiness to hear it whispered that Congress will not probably ratify the arrangements proposed for the benefit of the army. If we had as much virtue as we ought to have, this would produce no dangerous change; but according to the present interested ideas of men, many of our best officers will very likely retire from the service.

The whole corps of officers look up to the committee of Congress, and anxiously wait the result of their recommendations. The most disinterested lament the delay, and tremble for the cause of their country. My dearest friend and father, adieu.

I am your most affectionate

JOHN LAURENS.

The Honble Henry Laurens, Esqr.,

President of Congress, York.

(Private).

HEAD QUARTERS, *9th March*, 1778.

My Dear Father:

I have received your three letters, one of the 1st inst., and two of the 3[d], with the very seasonable supply of buff cloth, which, that I may not disgrace the relation in which I stand to the president of Congress, and the Commander in chief of the armies of the United States, by an unworthy appearance, shall be immediately converted to proper use. My obligation is the greater, as my want was more pressing, and I entreat your acceptance of due thanks. The necessity of the case can only plead my excuse for intruding such minutious objects on a mind filled with the interests of a great empire.

The method which you allude to, of procuring the necessary article in question, has been clandestinely practiced by many. The policy of continuing the law which prohibits this commerce, is disputed. It does not appear to me, that a connivance at it on the part of the states would importantly injure our own manufactories, or encourage those of Great Britain. How far it might be pernicious in draining us of specie, and in reducing the present slender resources which we have for supporting our prisoners among the enemy, I cannot pronounce. The greatest objection I think is, that our country people and soldiers would be debauched by this interest. It is probable that one of the principal marts of the continent has capitally suffered by fire, and that we shall more than ever find it expedient to relax the vigor of our first resolutions against all kind of commerce with the enemy.

The naval expedition in which some of our brave landsmen, you say, have embarked, will, I hope, be crowned with deserved success.

The accounts which you have heard of repeated successes of the enemy's parties have probably been exaggerated. The major superintending the Taylors, from the best accounts I have been able to gather from two of our soldiers, who made their escape, and concurrent circumstances, appears to me inexcusable. He had sufficient warning to have admitted of his posting his guard advantageously, and repelling the enemy with loss, in case they should have hazarded an assault.

The number of men unfit for duty by reason of their nakedness, the number sick in hospitals, and present under innoculation, certainly emaciate the effective column in our returns.

Similar causes, added to the severity of the season, have prevented our completing the works of the camp, in such a manner as would have been indispensably necessary if we had been engaged with a more alert and enterprising antagonist.

The repeated cavils of some general officers have driven the engineer in his own defence to substitute lines to redoubts in fortifying the camp, whereby the labor of the soldier was greatly augmented, and the extent to be mann'd is considerably increased. The position which we at present occupy, is not that which was at first judiciously chosen. The bridge over Schuylkil which was intended to be one of the avenues of retreat is so placed, that it is impossible to cover it by any work. Perhaps in case of attack, we shall be obliged to abandon both that and our huts, to the destroying hand of the enemy, and if we fight at all, must make a stand in the rear of both.

It is a very bad principle, to trust to the usual sluggishness and inactivity of the enemy. But when I reflect upon the great indulgence of Gen¹ Howe, I draw some consolation from hoping that he will not do violence to his nature by any extraordinary exertions at the present moment, but postpone his visit 'till we be better prepared for receiving him. These truths are deposited in the breasts of a few, and must be deplored in silence. But every prudent method and general argument should be used to stimulate the different states to the immediate completion of their regiments.

I am truly sensible of your kindness on the subject of my black battalion. Nothing would tempt me to quit my present station, but a prospect of being more useful in another.

The ambition of serving my country, and desire of gaining fame, leads me to wish for the command of men. I would cherish those dear, ragged Continentals, whose patience will be the admiration of future ages, and glory in bleeding with them.

It gives me the most serious concern, to find that you have any thoughts of retiring from Congress. That body collectively — it is a deplorable truth — has fallen into disrepute. Firm and disinterested patriots are more than ever wanted. I entreat you in the name of your country, not to lessen their numbers at this critical epoch of our affairs. I think the sum proposed might be very usefully disposed. The effect greatly depends upon a judicious distribution, and would be more certain if the sum could be augmented by other contributions. A gift of this kind, deposited in the hands of Mr. Franklin, at Philadelphia, might prove a blessing to the sick and naked. Blankets, and a few of the little articles which comfort disordered nature, would lessen the horrors of a goal, and keep our unhappy soldiers from despair.

The Baron Steuben has had the fortune to please uncommonly, for a stranger, at first sight.

All the gen¹ officers who have seen him, are prepossessed in his favor, and conceive highly of his abilities. I must tell you tho', by the bye, that Congress has mistaken his rank in Prussia. He was there *lieutenant general quartier maitre*, which in good English is deputy quarter master general. He had never any higher rank in the Prussian service, than that of colonel. But he was lieutenant general of the Margrave de Baden's troops, after he had retired from the Prussian army in disgust. As far as my line can

18

reach, I conceive the baron to be profound in the military science.

The General seems to have a very good opinion of him, and thinks he might be usefully employed in the office of inspector general, but I fancy is cautious of recommending it to Congress, as he might appear implacably to pursue a certain person to whom Congress gave that post. Now it is a doubt with me whether the gentleman in question was not virtually removed from the inspectorship by being ordered on the Canadian expedition. In that case, the difficulty would be obviated. The baron's own desire is to have for the present the rank and pay of major gen[l]; not to have any actual command, until he is better known, and shall be better qualified by a knowledge of our language, and the genius and manners of the people. Then, if any stroke is to be struck, his ambition prompts him to solicit a command.

Mrs. Washington has received the miniature, and wishes to know whether Major Rogers is still at York. The defects of this portrait I think are, that the visage is too long, and old age is too strongly marked in it. He is not altogether mistaken, with respect to the languor of the general's eye; for altho' his countenance when affected either by joy or anger, is full of expression, yet when the muscles are in a state of repose, his eye certainly wants animation. My proficiency in this kind of drawing never went beyond sketching a profile. I never attempted to paint a miniature likeness of a full face. There is a miniature painter in camp who has made two or three successful attempts to produce the general's likeness.

The indulgence granted to Gen¹ Burgoyne, I have no doubt will operate rather to our advantage, than otherwise. He is too much a man of the world not to have a convenient pliability, and therefore I am not surprised that in his present circumstances, he has paid homage to Congress.

Since the 1st of the month, we have had twenty-two deserters from the enemy, exclusive of those of our own soldiers, who, during their confinement, had been driven by unremitting inhumanity to enter their service, and embraced the first opportunity to escape. Of the latter class, so many have given them the slip immediately on receiving their new clothes, that Gen¹ Howe under pretence of paying the passages of our deserters to England, for their greater security against our pursuit, distributes them on board the fleet, where they will either be made seamen, or kept for the service of the islands, E. Indies, etc. By the accounts of deserters yesterday, it appears that the enemy have embarked, or are preparing to embark, a considerable number of invalids. The intelligence given by the majority of them confirms our ideas of the weak state of their regiments, and from Mr. Howe's characteristic caution almost ensures us against an attack before his reinforcements arrive.

We have the pleasure to be informed that the
recruiting service goes extremely well on in the Delaware state, and there are good prospects in the eastern
states of completing the regiments speedily.   You will
be informed of Capt Barry's success with two or three
armed boats on the Delaware.   Two transports loaded
with forage, one of them mounting six four pounders
attended by a schooner, mounting eight four pounders
and four howitzers, fell into his hands, by his gallantry and address.   The schooner had on board a
lieutenant of engineers and company of artificers,
some valuable intrenching tools, officers' baggage and
wines, delicacies destined for Genl Howe's table, etc.
Capt Barry was obliged to destroy the ships, and set
out on a new cruise with the schooner.   A large fleet
of the enemy's vessels were coming up the river.
Barry mantained an obstinate fight; his men once
leaped into the boat and were preparing to desert him :
his presence of mind and singular address recovered
them.   He renewed the combat, but surrounded and
overpowered, he was obliged to run his schooner on
shore, where he saved the cannon and every thing
valuable, and rendered the schooner useless.   You
may see that I write in great haste, which I am the
more sorry for, as it would give me pleasure to dwell
upon the praises due to Capt Barry.   Among other
things taken on board the schooner are a number of
German letters and papers relative to the foreign regiments in British service, from whence we hope to

gain some useful intelligence. Gen¹ Knyphausen's order of the Lion d'or is likewise taken, but will be sent unto him.

> I am ever your most affectionate
>
> > JOHN LAURENS.

With this you will receive a letter from Baron Steuben.

If among the books Duplessis has given you, there is one entitled *La Tactique de Ghibert*, I am very anxious to read it.

Likewise the work of Mesnil Durand.

> HEAD QUARTERS, 14*th March*, 1778.

My Dear Father:

This will be delivered to you by the Count Pulaski, whose prowess is not unknown to you.

The dislike of some of his officers to him as a stranger, the advantages which they have taken of him as such, and their constant contrivances to thwart him on every occasion, made it impossible for him to command with that satisfaction to himself and benefit to the public, which would undoubtedly have resulted from their acting in concert with him. He has therefore resigned his command, and determines to solicit Congress to entrust him with a legionary corps composed of 68 horse, and about 200 foot. With such a corps and proper officers under him, to be perpetually scouring the interval between the two armies, and embracing every opportunity for a stroke of partisanship, he thinks he will render considerable service, and I am persuaded from his intelligence and enterprising spirit, that the event will do him honour.

His military ardour is very great, and he is exceedingly uneasy, lest by any delay on the part of Congress he should be obliged to appear late in the field, which would be almost as painful to him as refusal in the first instance.

He apprehends no difficulty in raising his number of cavalry; to engage the quota of infantry will be almost impossible, unless Congress will make an exception in his favour to their resolution against the admission of prisoners and deserters into the service. This is warranted by the practice of other nations, and deserters, etc., enlisted in detached corps are not by any means so dangerous as if they were admitted in the line.

The count will be allowed, I presume, the Continental bounty for men, and the rate established for equipping his cavalry. His eagerness to distinguish himself will not suffer him to confine himself to the latter if he finds it inadequate.

He expects to retain his rank as brigadier. If his whole history were known, Congress would grant his request with thanks for his generous disinterestedness on the present occasion.

I beg leave to introduce the Count to your acquaintance; you may depend upon it that Congress will not have reason to repent of having employed him in the way which is proposed.

His zeal for our cause and courage, proof against every danger will cover him with glory, and I hope promote the general interest.

I am your most affectionate

JOHN LAURENS.

The Honble Henry Laurens, Esqr.,

President of Congress, York.

Fav^d by Briga^d General Count Pulaski.

HEAD QUARTERS, 22*d March*, 1778.

My Dear Father:

This will be delivered to you by Brigadier General Du Portail, commanding officer of Engineers, whom I am glad of having an opportunity of introducing to your acquaintance. His knowledge of his profession renders him respectable, and by aiding his want of fluency in the English, with your French, you will find his conversation agreeable and worth attending to.

I do not know whether what I am going to solicit can be effected, nor would I ask it if it were anything contrary to rule, or that could be productive of the most remote ill consequences. Mr. De Murnant, a French gentleman, offered himself as assistant engineer, under strong recommendations from Gen¹ Du Portail. His excellency submitted the matter to the committee in camp, and it is very probable that in the order of business it might not present itself till very late for the ratification of Congress. In the mean time, the poor man is kept in a state of suspense, and what is equally bad, of expence. If the question relative to him could be brought on the carpet immediately, as it cannot be a subject of long debate or occasion any interruption to business, Gen¹ Du Portail and himself wish that it may be done. He is at present employed in works of the camp.

I must not defer thanking you for your kind letter of the 15th inst. Tho' I am unable to give such answer to it as you wish, I still hope that the arguments which you use on the subject of your retiring from Congress, will be seen in another light.

Du Plessis told me that he had commissioned a Mr. De la Balme to put some books into your hands for me. My dearest friend and father, adieu.

                    Ever your affectionate

                            JOHN LAURENS.

The Honble Henry Laurens, Esqr.,

        President of Congress, York.

    Favd by Gen¹ Du Portail.

HEAD QUARTERS, 25*th March*, 1778.

I was obliged to write you a hurried letter by the hands of Gen¹ Du Portail and had barely time to acknowledge the receipt of your favour of the 15ᵗʰ. Yesterday I had the pleasure of receiving your kind letter of the 22ᵈ with Sº. Carolina papers and letters from England. Among them was the enclosed for you, which I take to be from my wife. Her last date to me is the 1ˢᵗ November, at which time she and your granddaughter were well. I enclose you likewise the last letter from Mr. Manning, the others were all of old dates. As Gen¹ McIntosh is ordered with a detachment on the other side Schuylkil, to cover the passage of a large drove of cattle that have crossed the Delaware at Sherard's ferry, I take the liberty of detaining the N. papers till his return, which will be in a day or two, that he may not miss what will be so great a treat to him. He has mentioned to me several times of late, that he fancied you were retaliating his ancient delinquencies.

I am grieved that you persevere in your resolution of retiring from Congress. Your reelection is a testimony of the good opinion of your countrymen, and I think it is needless to urge the necessity of increasing rather than diminishing the number of able and virtuous men in the grand council of the nation.

The retiring of a single one at the present crisis

19

is a dangerous example, and may fatally strengthen the hands of those who have not the cause of liberty and the interest of their country at heart. I have long anxiously desired to see you, but the unabating flow of business in the general's family restrained me from asking leave. Two of our gentlemen[1] are appointed commissioners to meet General Howe at German Town, for negociating the exchange of prisoners. Their absence will render the presence of the rest more than ever necessary; but if you will give me notice when it will be convenient for me to come, I will ask for a short furlough, that I may have the happiness of embracing you, and saying many things which are not so well expressed in writing.

The Baron Steuben has commenced the functions of inspector general. Several officers whose character and abilities give them influence, and are pledges of success, are to be nominated as sub-inspectors; intelligent active men are appointed to each brigade to serve as brigade inspectors. The baron has given some elementary lessons in writing, preparatory to ulterior instructions; and we hope by this institution that the important end of establishing uniformity of discipline and manoeuvres throughout the army will be accomplished.

This I communicate to yourself only, for I don't

---

[1] Colonels Harrison and Hamilton.

know whether the general communicates this plan by this courier for ratification.

The baron discovers the greatest zeal, and an activity which is hardly to be expected at his years. The officers in general seem to entertain a high opinion of him, and he sets them an excellent example in descending to the functions of a drill-sergeant.

A French gentleman of the name of Ternant with whom I was slightly acquainted at the cape François, is arrived in camp, and offers himself as one of the sub-inspectors. His talents qualify him in a superior degree for the office. He has travelled so much as to have worn off the characteristic manners of his nation, and he speaks our language uncommonly well.

The baron is very desirous of having him as an assistant, and says he is persuaded he will be an acquisition to the States. The only thing against him is, that he comes without recommendatory letters. The Congress have I think very wisely resolved against employing any more foreigners unless they are forced to it by the special contracts of their embassadors, or very pointed recommendations. On this account the General has, in order that the baron might not lose so good an assistant, put the matter upon this footing: that Mr. Ternant may exercise the office of sub-inspector without rank for the present; and that when his practical abilities are as well known as his theo-

retical, Congress will determine a rank suitable to his
merit. It is to be observed that he studied engineer-
ing particularly, and would have wished to join the
corps here, but party differences were an invincible
obstacle. He has not, however, confined his views to
that branch of military science, but seems to be equally
well instructed in every other.

If an exception to the generally established rule is
ever to be made, I think it can never be with more
propriety than in favour of a person who merits such
qualifications.

The baron desires his friendly compliments to you.
Apropos to him, his secretary, and a Mon^r de Pon-
tieres have certificates signed by the president of
Congress setting forth that they are to have the rank
of captains.

I think they were not announced as such to the
General. Baron Steuben's secretary is desirous of
drawing his pay, and upon application to the General,
who is not explicitly acquainted with the intentions of
Congress in this matter, was required to draw on
account. This has created some uneasiness in the
Baron's mind, and he wishes to know whether Mr.
Duponceau is not entitled to the pay, as well as rank
of captain.

I think if I could have half an hour's conversation
with you, my dear father, I could prove to you so
clearly how much the public interest is concerned in
your remaining in Congress, that you would not

refuse yourself to this duty. Anticipating the pleasure
of embracing you, I am, my dear father,

> Your most affectionate
>
> JOHN LAURENS.

The Honble Henry Laurens, Esqr.,

> President of Congress, York.

(Private).

HEAD QUARTERS, 28*th March*, 1778.

Last night General McIntosh returned with the
agreeable intelligence that the supply of cattle which
he was ordered to protect was out of danger.

He received the S°. Carolina newspapers in ecstacy,
and we had some serious conversation together upon
the subject of your retiring from Congress, in which
we determined that your presence in that assembly is
more necessary now, than it would have been at any
other period since the revolution. More judgment,
more spirit, more firmness in the conduct of the
political bark are required than ever. So far are we
from thinking that your service may be dispensed
with on account of the appointment of the other dele-
gates from S°. Carolina, that we judge it more pecu-
liarly incumbent on you, in consequence of the choice
of one whose great talents, from a defect of probity,
render him the more dangerous to remain a guardian
of the liberties of these rising States; and not by your

absence to strengthen the party of men who make their individual selves the centre of the universe.

I conjure you, my dearest friend and father, in the name of your country, not to leave the fate of this empire, this last asylum of liberty, at their disposal. Every one of your letters, in which you so pathetically describe the low ebb of patriotism, furnishes me with irrefutable arguments.

You do not particularly mention your reasons for quitting the Congress at this time. Impaired health, diminution of property and other reasons which have their weight might be urged, but what can be put in competition with the object of your present labours.

I am happy to hear that Congress is about to reward Captain Lee of the dragoons for his distinguished services. His brilliant actions have been so frequent, that I think their decision need not be preceded by much deliberation.

Nothing but his own modesty has prevented his being recommended to the notice of Congress long since. This officer only wants a larger sphere of action to show the extent of his military talents, and it will be for the benefit of the service, as well as a piece of justice to entrust him with a larger command, and honour him with a higher rank. The presence of disinterested patriots is wanted, if it were only to patronize real merit, and oppose the sudden rise of persons who have nothing but connections and family interest to recommend them.

From some accounts lately received, it appears that Gen¹ Howe is concentrating his forces. Such of his transports as are at sea will be much exposed to the dangers of a lee-shore, by the storm of eastern wind which seems to increase every moment. The advantage which he will have over us, if his transports are safe, and have tolerable passages will be, a power of taking the field earlier than we can. If he would do us the favour of attacking us in the position we are now fortifying, we might safely allow him a superiority of numbers. But we must have our tents early, for in case of attack, we must sacrifice our huts.

This goes under the care of Brigadier Gen¹ Woodford, who is proceeding to Virginia on public and private business.

With the tenderest affection, your dutiful son.

JOHN LAURENS.

HEAD QUARTERS, 1st *April*, 1778.

My dear Father:

I have received your kind favour of yesterday, inclosing a letter from Stephorsts at Amsterdam, which served as a cover to a letter from my wife, of the 23ᵈ October, in which she informs me that my uncle and family were shortly expected in London, to take leave of their friends, previous to setting out for the south of France.

Deserters and inhabitants from Philadelphia say that there are no troops arrived there, except a few German convalescents from New York. Neither does it appear by their accounts that the large fleet mentioned by General Smallwood, which probably consists of victuallers and forage ships, is arrived yet at the city.

Our commissioners proceeded yesterday morning to German Town according to agreement, and a strict neutrality and suspension of hostilities are to be observed in all the extent of the village during the conference. The English commissioners, I am informed, returned to town last night. If they intend to do so every night, they will have the advantage of constant and more minute consultations with their principal.

I must not omit to inform you that Baron Steuben is making a sensible progress with our soldiers. The officers seem to have a high opinion of him, and discover a docility from which we may augur the most happy effects.

It would enchant you to see the enlivened scene of our Campus Martius. If Mr. Howe opens the campaign with his usual deliberation, and our recruits or draughts come in tolerably well, we shall be infinitely better prepared to meet him, than ever we have been.

Mr. Francis, who will deliver you this, takes charge likewise of your Carolina newspapers.

He speaks of you in terms of such high respect,

as are exceedingly grateful to one who is so devoted
to you as your

JOHN LAURENS.

I inclose you a billet which I received this morning
from Bringhurst.

The Honble Henry Laurens, Esqr.,
    President of Congress, York.

(Private).

HEAD QUARTERS, 5th April, 1778.

My Dear Father:

I have barely time to thank you for your kind letter
accompanied by the speech and letter of President
Rutledge, on the subject of his resignation. As I
have not found a leisure moment proper for submit-
ting them to the perusal of the General, I take the
liberty of detaining them 'till another opportunity
offers.

In the mean time, I have in general terms communicated the intelligence to his Excellency.

My opinion was formed immediately upon reading
the matter over. I certainly think Mr. President is
right in the principle which he lays down relative to
the limited powers of those to whom the people have
committed that Constitution, by which they wish to be
governed. They are to make laws conformably to
the Constitution, but they have no authority to alter

or change the Constitution. I disagree with him when he makes our present form of government have such an absolute respect to an accommodation with G^t Britain, and when he declares the present Constitution of S^o. Carolina to be the best we are capable of receiving; but I hope to have time to speak more fully on this subject in my next.

The conduct of Congress in giving orders to officers on detached commands, without communicating them to the General, is not only a deficiency of politeness, considered as an omission of a compliment which is due to him, but likewise a breach of military propriety. He ought undoubtedly to be acquainted with whatever orders are given to those who are at the same time under his command, that he may govern himself by them and not be exposed to contrariate them. We expect the pleasure of Genl Lee's company to dinner, and are preparing to receive him with distinction.

Adieu, my dearest friend and father.

I am ever your affectionate

JOHN LAURENS.

The Honble Henry Laurens, Esqr.,
        President of Congress, York.
    (Private).

HEAD QUARTERS, 11*th April*, 1778.

My Dear Father:

I have read with attention your kind favour of the 2ᵈ inst., and have frequently had occasion to discuss the subject matter of it. I have more than once contended, that supposing the Congress should be guilty of the greatest injustice towards the officers of the army, a general abandonment of the service at this perilous crisis, the consequences of which must evidently be the ruin of our cause, would merit eternal infamy. A majority, composed perhaps only of ten men, conduct the present system, will you, to punish them for acting either unadvisedly or even with ill design, sacrifice the liberties of America, and desperately involve yourselves in the perdition which you bring upon them? That man, however injured by the representatives of the people, who will desert the public interest, is destitute of virtue and unworthy to be free.

I must confess to you, with grief, my dearest friend, that upon a nearer view, I have a far less respectable idea of my countrymen than when I beheld their struggle from afar, and could not distinguish the vices with which they are oppressed. I was thunderstruck at hearing a system adopted of governing men by their vices, and putting public virtue and patriotism out of the question, as nonentities, a system so subversive of republicanism that if it prevails, we may bid adieu to our liberties.

Before I received your letter, I was generally against the pensionary half pay establishment, but had not seen in their full extent the inconveniences that would arise from it. You have developed some ideas that had but slightly and feebly presented themselves to me, and have confirmed my opinion; but, at the same time that I require such virtue in those of the army, as to esteem the loss of estate a cheap price to pay for the honour of establishing the liberties of their country, I would wish the burthens of society as equally distributed as possible, that there may not be one part of the community appropriating to itself the summit of wealth and grandeur, while another is reduced to extreme indigence in the common cause. By what means this is to be effected wise legislators must determine. The power of our enemies and their perfection in the military science, opposed to our inexperience, seem to render it impolitic to arrive at this by alternation in military service. Our safety requires that we should retain those officers and soldiers who are most enured to arms, in order to oppose veterans. Can it be effected by taxes on luxuries, which would be felt only by the rich? In a republic there ought to be the penalties of sumptuary laws, and should be so severe as to amount to a prohibition; consequently no fund could be established by these means, to answer any extensive purpose.

If we were as virtuous as we ought to be, we should have those who are enriching themselves by commerce, privateering and farming, supplying the army with every necessary convenience at a moderate rate; but as experience proves that it is in vain to expect this, all I would demand of Congress, is that they would contrive some means of furnishing us with articles which nature cannot forego, and which are useful in giving respectability to the military state, at such prices as bear some proportion to our pay.

I would wish to see the military state rendered honorable, and all odious distinctions of jealousy laid aside, for we are all citizens, and have no separate interests. If mediocrity could be established generally, by any means, it would be well; it would ensure us virtue and render our independency permanent. But there never will be virtue in the poor, when there are rich in the same community. By imperceptible and indirect methods, we should labour to establish and maintain equality of fortunes as much as possible, if we would continue to be free.

It is a fact that our officers cannot satisfy the simple wants of nature, much less make that appearance which is annexed to the military state, with their pay. It is no less a fact that in every town on the continent, luxury flourishes as it would among a people who had conquered the world, and were about to pay for their victories, by their decline. This I hope Congress will take seriously into consideration.

I would by no means wish our pay to be increased, but I would wish to see temptations to peculation in weak men removed, and the honest man delivered from the necessity of reducing himself to beggary. This will best be effected by a public establishment for supplying wants at a moderate price.

I have received your favour, inclosing a note for Bringhurst, which will be sent to him by the first good opportunity.

Your favour of the 9th is just received, with the blue cloth and the buttons, for which I return you my best thanks. The last paragraph makes me the more uneasy, as I do not know in what way we are menaced and what is the extent of the danger.

We have heard nothing from our commissioners since their arrival at New Town, from whence we conclude that they are going on well. They were exceedingly chagrined at the distrust of their abilities which was conspicuous in the resolves of Congress. They had been perfectly satisfied with the prospects which they had at their first interview, at German Town.

Inclosed you will receive the Rutledge papers. The General has been so much occupied that I have not given them him to read, and though he has got over his great business of a long official letter, I fear to detain them any longer. Altho' he is an advocate for the half pay establishment, on the principles of economy and justice to the officers, I apprehend that if any other mode were proposed for rendering commissions honorable, and enabling the officers to subsist with decency, he is not inviolably attached to this.

Your most affectionate

JOHN LAURENS.

My best respects to Mr. Drayton; I will be looking out for quarters for him.

The Honble Henry Laurens, Esqr.,

President of Congress, York.

(Private).

HEAD QUARTERS, 18*th April*, 1778.

My Dear Father:

I have barely time to inclose you a Philadelphia paper and to thank you for the epaulettes which you were so kind as to send me.

The General sends you a handbill which has been artfully thrown out by the enemy, and which, unless properly counteracted, will undubitably tend to foment disunion, perhaps the only and evidently the surest method of destroying us. The deserters who have come in lately say it is a common talk that overtures are to be made for a treaty of peace. Capt Gibbes of the General's guard is now at Lancaster, and I have employed him to purchase me summer wear. My want of it will depend upon his success. However, if

what is at York is very good, I shall be very glad to
have as much as will make a skirtless waistcoat and a
pair of breeches.

With respect to the spurs which you have been so
kind as to take so much trouble about, my reason for
desiring James to have them changed was on account
of their weakness. Being all silver they are apt to
break; and I imagined that he might without difficulty exchange them for a pair of plated. If he can
not, he must get them mended and I must use them
tenderly.

Apropos to spurs, I think in the present deplorable
scarcity of good horses, it would be a very acceptable
present to the Baron Steuben on the part of Congress
to give him an elegant saddle horse. He is exerting
himself like a lieutenant anxious for promotion, and
the good effects of his labour are visible.

The General I apprehend is restrained from writing
to Congress on this head till he shall be acquainted
with the sentiments of the brigadiers respecting the
Baron's rank (but this between ourselves), as far as I
can learn in conversation with those gentlemen, every
one is convinced of his zeal and abilities, and thinks
him deserving of the grade which he asks for.

Praying your indulgence for this hurried and
almost illegible production,

I assure you of my constant love.

JOHN LAURENS.

" All our foreign publications seem to regard an

European war, as a certain consequence of the Elector of Bavaria's death.

"Mr. R. Strettle Jones, an ostensible and a very intelligent man, writes from Philadelphia to a friend of his in the army that Lord Chatham was certainly at the head of administration. '

"The reports of a French war tho' stifled as much as possible are generally believed."

HEAD QUARTERS, 20*th April*, 1778.
My Dear Father:

You will receive by this courier, Ld North's recantation. It would make an admirable contrast with a vehement oration which I heard him pronounce in the confidence of success, while I was in England. The treachery which he renounces is too palpable in his conciliatory overtures, to deceive thinking men; but they may prove a fatal poison if suffered to be disseminated through the continent, unattended by the strictures of an able pen, which may serve as an antidote. If France has not declared war, she does not merit our alliance; but I think it is more than probable that the sword has been drawn by this time in Europe. There is no doubt of Genl Howe's being recalled, and that Clinton is to succeed him. The present moment requires vigorous counsels and uncommon management.

21

I have many fears relative to our prospects of the ensuing campaign; they shall be expressed in a short letter. My dearest friend adieu.

Virtue and vigorous counsels with policy, are more wanted than ever.

Your affectionate
JOHN LAURENS.

I fear the effects of northern expeditions and projects. Our main army will be emacerated, and nothing decisive will be done. Let us be respectable in the field, and have a full representation of the wisest patriots.

HEAD QUARTERS, 27th April, 1778.

My Dear Father:

I have read with pleasure the report of the committee of Congress, on the subject of the insulting and insidious overtures made by the British ministers, tho' I think more firmness and energy would have made it more republican. The pardons offered to the subjects of the states who had embraced the party of the enemy, will, I am persuaded, be attended with extensive good consequences. The measure is dictated by policy, and unites the advantage of being founded in humanity. A few copies of the handbill have been sent to Governor Tryon in return for the triplicate packets of the British bill which he was so obliging as to send to the Commander in Chief. It appears to me that this proceeding of Ld North will be the signal for France to declare war. The reducing the commerce and naval power of her natural enemy, increasing her own, and humbling an inveterate rival, are objects too important in a political view, for her to hazard them to the wiles of negociation after they have been secured from the chance of war. This apart, the death of the Elector of Bavaria, it is generally thought will embroil Europe. And if our men in power, and men of influence, will redouble their exertions instead of being lulled into security, the new and artful attack of the British minister, will be foiled and expose him to contempt. He will be obliged to withdraw his troops — I mean as many of them as we suffer to escape — and tacitly to acknowledge what he will be afterwards forced explicitly to ratify — our independence. At the same time, if no secret alliance has been entered into on our part with France, our agents at that court need not represent it as an impossible event, that a treaty should take place between Great Britain and America, from the degree of affection which may still remain between the two nations and the propensity to a connexion which arises from the indentity of habits and language.

I have been informed that the tone of our embassadors was infinitely too modest to produce the effects which we had a right to expect.

It gives me pleasure to find that Congress has

directed General Gates to have a conference with
Gen¹ Washington previous to his setting out for his
northern command. A proper force kept up in the
neighbourhood of New York, provided it can be done
without prejudice to this army, may be attended with
very important good consequences.

It is a favourite plan with some men, to make a
sudden attempt in that quarter with a part of this
army, and change the theatre of the war; but there
are many irrefragable arguments against the project.
Their plan is to carry that city by storm; but the
preliminary steps to be taken, and the length of march
would inevitably betray the design. The part of the
army left here would be attacked and dissipated by
a superior force. The British army would be re-
cruited from among the numerous disaffected, which
swarm in this state, and the force before New York,
if sufficient to proceed by regular approaches, would
be obliged to raise the siege with disgrace, upon reinforcements being thrown in, which might very well
be spared from Philadelphia; besides, as New York,
supposing it carried, cannot be maintained while the
enemy have the superiority by sea, it can by no means
deserve to be made a principal object of attention.
But if we are sufficiently strengthened here to act
offensively, and a respectable force is posted in the
vicinity of N. York, we may hope for decisive success, and we avoid the risk of suffering the enemy to
establish themselves, and strengthen their party in

this state; cut off the communication between the northern and southern states, and reduce the Congress to the disgraceful necessity of decamping a second time. I say nothing of the unavoidable loss of stores, whatever diligence may be used in removing them.

I must ask, my dear father, a thousand pardons for this ill-digested and incoherent letter. I set out with a good intention, but from my first beginning it 'till now, I have undergone perpetual interruption.

Capᵗ Gibbes has disappointed me in not purchasing the stuff for summer wear. I must entreat you to let James procure me as much as will make two or three changes, provided the extravagance of the price does not forbid it.

Adieu my dearest friend and father,

JOHN LAURENS.

I send a letter which you will be so good as to inclose by Mr. Francis, to Coˡ Gervaise, to be forwarded.

HEAD QUARTERS, 1st May, 1778.

I snatch a minute to congratulate my dear father, upon the important intelligence from France. As the matter is represented she seems to have acted with politic generosity towards us, and to have timed her declaration in our favour most admirably for her own interests, and the abasement of her ancient rival. If the general languor can be shaken off, and that this

event instead of increasing our supineness stimulates
us to vigorous exertions, we may close the war with
great eclat, provided General Howe does not receive
timely orders to collect his force and secure a retreat.
France might give a mortal blow to the English naval
force in its present scattered state.

I have just received your kind favour of the 28th
ult°. I have reason to hope that opportunities for
writing to my wife will be more frequent and certain,
and that we may soon find a proper conveyance for
herself.

With respect to the report of the committee, I think
a more spirited answer was required to the arrogance
and insolence of the British minister in offering us
pardons, and a part of our rights. I am entirely of
your opinion on the subject of the proposed addition
to the resolutions.

The only reason that can be assigned for Col.
Hartley's delay, is that there are better quarters at
York than at Valley Forge. The General probably is
ignorant that he has received his order to march from
Congress.

General McIntosh desires me to send you the
inclosed paper, with his compliments.

Your letter to Bringhurst went some time since.
I received an answer from him a day or two ago, that
the body of your carriage is at the painter's in Philadelphia, and that if I give him a pass for a gentleman
who wants to get a carriage in, that gentleman will

undertake to get a pass for yours to come out. I must inquire who the gentleman is, and if the matter can be transacted with propriety it shall be done. He promises to finish the carriage out of hand, if this arrangement can be made.

I am hurried to close my letter, and must bid adieu to my dear father.

JOHN LAURENS.

HEAD QUARTERS, *4th May*, 1778.

I thank you my dear father for your kind favour of yesterday, and again congratulate you upon the important intelligence from France. It seems to me to have been her interest to offer such generous terms to America, as to ensure her prompt acceptance, and to avoid every thing which might give room for deliberation and delay. If our embassadors in France were plenipotentiaries, the ratification comes of course. If they were not, I think it is as little politic as generous to refuse an alliance with France in order to accept one upon equal terms with Great Britain.

There is still a prejudice in the minds of many people in favour of the latter, which should be wisely counteracted, or that power will gain by artful policy what she has lost in the field of battle. The intelligence seems to diffuse sincere joy. We only wait for leave from Congress to signify that of the army, by sounds which will reach the ears of the enemy.

My wife writes that my uncle is at Marseilles; his stay there depends entirely on my aunt. Harry at Richmond, and wrote letters which I have never received.

Mrs. Savage died at Brompton, three weeks before the date of the letter, which is 17th Feb^y, 1778.

Lady Willm Campbell had paid my wife a visit. What was the end of that unexpected civility, does not strike me.

Your grand-daughter and Mr. Manning's family were well, and desired their love.

It has been my ill fortune to write all my letters for some time past in very great haste, and this is the case at present, when I would particularly have wished to write deliberately.

Your most affectionate
JOHN LAURENS.

P.S. I am desired to request that you will send more blank forms of oaths.

HEAD QUARTERS, 7th May, 1778.

My Dear Father:

I have to ask pardon for omitting in my last, to thank you for the striped dimity, which you were so kind as to send me. It did not occur to me 'till it was too late to recall the messenger, and my uneasiness was the greater, as I had been frequently a delinquent in this way.

Yesterday we celebrated the new alliance, with as much splendour as the short notice would allow. Divine service preceded the rejoicing. After a proper pause, the several brigades marched by their right to their posts in order of battle, and the line was formed with admirable rapidity and precision. Three salutes of artillery, thirteen each, and three general discharges of a running fire by the musquetry, were given in honour of the king of France, the friendly European powers, and the United American States. Loud huzzas!

The order with which the whole was conducted, the beautiful effect of the running fire, which was executed to perfection, the martial appearance of the troops, gave sensible pleasure to every one present. The whole was managed by signal, and the plan, as formed by Baron de Steuben, succeeded in every particular, which is in a great measure attributed to his unwearied attention, and to the visible progress which the troops have already made, under his discipline.

A cold collation was given afterwards, at which all the officers of the army, and some ladies of the neighbourhood were present. Triumph beamed in every countenance. The greatness of mind and policy of Louis XVI were extol^d, and his long life toasted with as much sincerity as that of the British king used to

22

be in former times. The General received such proofs of the love and attachment of his officers as must have given him the most exquisite feelings.

But amid all this inundation of joy, there is a conduct observed towards him by certain great men which, as it is humiliating, must abate his happiness. I write with all the freedom of a person addressing himself to his dearest friend, and with all the unconstraint of a person delivering an unconsequential private opinion. I think, then, the Commander in Chief of this army is not sufficiently informed of all that is known by Congress of European affairs. Is it not a galling circumstance, for him to collect the most important intelligence piece-meal, and as they choose to give it, from gentlemen who come from York? Apart the chagrin which he must necessarily feel at such an appearance of slight, it should be considered that in order to settle his plan of operations for the ensuing campaign, he should take into view the present state of European affairs, and Congress should not leave him in the dark.

If ever there was a man in the world whose moderation and patriotism fitted him for the command of a republican army, he is, and he merits an unrestrained confidence.

You will receive copies of letters from and to the general, respecting Monsieur de Neuville. If I recollect right, that gentleman aims at the rank of brigadier. This, I can venture to assure you, the general does not think either politic or proper to be granted to him. I took the liberty of mentioning this, that the General's letter which is couched in polite terms, might not induce an opinion of his approving the demands of M. de la Neuville. The general thinks him a man of merit and liberal sentiments, but that he looks too high. I take the liberty which is allowed when the restraint of officiality is laid, to say many things which cannot with propriety be said in public letters. And am with as much respect for you in your public capacity, as love and friendship in our private relation,

Your

JOHN LAURENS.

HEAD QUARTERS, 12th May, 1778.

My Dear Father:

I felicitate you upon the declaration of war between England and France; for though we have no positive intelligence of the event, its immediate and sure precursors have taken place, from whence we may fairly conclude that it has followed in due course. The sarcastical declaration of Monsr de Noailles, proves the contempt which the French have for the British power in its present dismembered state, their confidence in their own strength seconded by that of their own allies, and is the most humiliating stroke that the national pride of Britain ever suffered. If

she is not instantly driven to negotiate a disgraceful
peace, she must principally depend upon powerful
naval exertions.   Her superiority in this kind of war,
might gain her great advantages, and in some degree
reestablish her affairs, were not American privateers,
and the rising Continental army in the opposite scale.
Ld North talks of new levies for internal defence.
The idea of reinforcements to act offensively in America seems to be dropped.   Indeed, my private
opinion is, that Sr Wm Howe or Sr Harry Clinton
has received orders to evacuate Philadelphia after
doing as much mischief as possible.   The great preparations which are making for a grand exhibition of
pageantry, if it be true as it is said, that a new build-
ing which is now rising is intended for a ceremony
relative to the order of knighthood, and every kind of
show that is made of a design to remain in Philadelphia, rather confirm than shake my opinion.

It gives me concern that there is no immediate prospect of closing the war with brilliancy.   A successful
general action, or some happy stroke upon one of
the important points of which the enemy are at present in possession, would be very desirable, as it
would clearly establish the military reputation of our
country, render us more independent of our allies,
raise the character of our General, and give all young
soldiers one more opportunity of distinguishing themselves in the dear cause of their country.

I heard by mere accident from General St Clair

that the legislative powers had ventured to alter the constitution of S° Carolina, that it is now degenerated into an aristocracy. This has occasioned no less surprise than unhappiness in my mind. I should not have imagined that in a country where the people are generally enlightened, and of an independent spirit, we should have suffered the depositaries of our constitution to usurp a power which is inherent only in the people, and to have corrupted what they were delegated to preserve. If this passes with impunity, the same men may next vote themselves perpetual representatives of the people. A few men of powerful influence may next have credit enough to take all government into their own hands. To an oligarchy succeeds a monarchy, limited by a few checks, which may be easily removed by an artful prince, and make way for despotism. It will be said that the confederate states, and the temper of the Carolinians themselves, would never suffer corruption to go such lengths; but I only observe that it is of the most fatal tendency to suffer fundamental principles to be violated, and that the measures taken by our present representatives are subversive of liberty. If your leisure will permit, I entreat to send me some account of these transactions, or perhaps I shall be able to get it from Mr Drayton, who, I understand, is on his way to camp.

The general officers are just now assembled to take the oath of allegiance.

The independent States of America will have the first oath that ever I took. As this matter is intended for the vulgar, I think it a pity that more solemnity and awe is not attached to the ceremony.

My dearest friend and father I tenderly embrace you.

JOHN LAURENS.

HEAD QUARTERS, 27th May, 1778.

My Dear Father:

I was obliged to break off abruptly in my last letter and send it unfinished. To resume the thread of narration will be hardly possible; indeed it would not be worth troubling you with, as you must have heard before this time of the principal circumstances of our retreat, and the failure of the British disposition. Generals Clinton and Howe were both out with the whole army, deducting the necessary guards for the city. One of the columns executed a march of 35 miles which proved fatal to several of their plethoric soldiers.

The Marquis made a brilliant retreat, and left the surrounding enemy to return to the city with precipitation. The firing of our alarm guns at camp, the crossing a few troops at Sullivan's bridge, and the report of a great number, added to the good order in which the detachment retired, saved the flower of our army. We have since seen a Philadelphia *Gazette* in which our detachment is called a large body of the rebels, their number covered under the appellation of a detachment. The Marquis is said to have retreated in the greatest confusion, and the party that crossed the Schuylkil here are said to have recrossed panic struck, and to have taken up the bridge after them. In the same *Gazette* there is a pompous description of the medley of entertainments which the city had given in testimony of their affection for General Howe; they call it a mischianza (pronounce miskiansa) which is an Italian word signifying a medley.

The most recent intelligence from Philadelphia is, that the troops drew yesterday three days provision and had their canteens filled with rum, that the women and children had embarked, some of the sick had been removed from the hospital and bettering house, the spare bedding and hospital utensils had been shipped, boxes of arms numbered were removing from the arsenal to the vessels. Coffin and Anderson, a capital Tory house, were packing up their merchandise.

The number of transports amounted to 180 vessels, averaging 250 tons each. This does not appear adequate to the number of troops, &ca., and makes us think that the enemy will retreat through the Jerseys, after embarking their heavy cannon and baggage, the horses belonging to them, their invalids and their new levies, whose desertion they have good reason to dread.

We learn farther, that notice was given on Saturday
to the officers of police, that the army was about
to remove, and that vessels were prepared for such
families as should choose to quit the city — that there
was a general despair among the Tory inhabitants —
that the enemy were still at work on their new
redoubts.

On Sunday the command devolved to General
Clinton. Gen¹ Howe took leave of the city and dined
with his brother on board of the Eagle.

The inhabitants anxious to know whether their
persons and property will be protected from the rage
of the American soldiery — if they could be sure of
protection, it is thought that much valuable merchandise would be retained in the city, which otherwise
will be sent away.

The greatest part of this intelligence was given by
a Mr. Combes, father of the clergyman — the old
gentleman is come out to make his peace and take
the oath — he will be sent back to town, with consolation for repentant sinners. Deserters, townsmen,
women of different qualities, spies, confirm the sub-
stance of these accounts. There has been such
diligence used in shipping, that some light carts
have been drawn by soldiers. Every kind of carriage
from waggons to wheelbarrows, have been incessantly rolling between the houses and water side for
some days past.

It is not certainly known whether they will embark

or march through the Jerseys; by the latter method of retiring they would avoid the dangers of the sea and a French fleet, economize provision and forage, be sure of arriving at New York at a given time; by the former they would be secure from desertion, and harrassing from such light troops as might be detached after them on their march; but the matter is put out of doubt, if what we have just heard from Col. Shreve, commandant in Jersey, be true, that several troops of the enemy's horse have embarked. This being the case, they certainly mean to go by sea, as every dragoon that can be mustered would be wanted in their march through the Jerseys.

Col. Shreve adds that the refugees are daily deserting from Billingsport, and surrendering themselves to the civil power, that several companies of artillery have embarked.

The intelligence from New York is that the enemy have abandoned Fort Washington and its dependencies. Whether their design is to concenter their force at New York, and make a stand there, or only rendezvous there to proceed elsewhere, or divide the force that they have at Philadelphia, part to go to reinforce New York, and part for the defence of their W. India islands, cannot be determined. It is certain that a notion prevails among the soldiery that many of them are going to the West Indies, and that immense desertion would take place if any opportunity were given.

23

God bless you, my dear father; I salute you with my tenderest love.

JOHN LAURENS.

The Honble Henry Laurens, Esqr.,
    President of Congress, York.

HEAD QUARTERS, *9th June*, 1778.

My Dear Father:

The moment Mr Boudinot returned from German Town where he had a conference with Mr Loring, British comm^y of prisoners, upon the subject of an exchange. He brings us intelligence that the commissioners appointed by act of Parliament to divide us by governor's places, &ca., skilfully dealt, are arrived; that they are, as we had heard Ld Carlisle, Gov. Johnston, and Mr Eden; that Ld Cornwallis is come with them. A spy of ours who left the city this morning says, that they landed at 2 o'clock yesterday afternoon, and that they came up the river in barges; that five or six hundred sailors had come up to the city in boats, and were assembled at the proper place for conducting the passage of the troops; that no ships remained near the town except the Vigilant and Richmond, who seem destined to cover the crossing, and that all the enemy's sick are removed.

Some people are of opinion that the arrival of the commissioners at Philadelphia is a proof that war is not yet declared between England and France; the former determining to try what may be done with respect to America, by the means of negotiation, and preferring in the mean time a suffering of inconveniences and insults, to engage at once in so unequal a contest; and that the commissioners have ventured to land in Philadelphia from a persuasion that a declaration of war will not originate with France.

It is certain that the commissioners must know whether war is declared, and it appears to me almost certain that they would not come to Philadelphia if it were. At all events I imagine the arrival of the commissioners will delay the final evacuation of the city 'till a council of war can be held, and perhaps some message sent to Congress. It would be an awkward appearance for them to arrive at Philadelphia with a view of proposing terms of conciliation, and to change their ground without announcing themselves. But it w^d be full as awkward and disgraceful for them to announce themselves and disappear before an answer from Congress could be given. All which inclines me to believe that war was not declared at the time they left England, and that their stay will be deferred by their court as long as possible. A deserter who is just arrived, says that none but the light troops remained in Philadelphia. Orders had been given for their preparing every thing for moving, but the arrival of the commissioners had occasioned a countermand.

Our treaty with France is known; what the commissioners can hope from their act of Parliament, which is an insult to our honour and understanding, I cannot conceive. Commissary Loring told Mr Boudinot with a grave face, that a fleet of forty ships had sailed from the British coast and struck such an alarm in the minds of the French king and his ministers as occasioned them to desire the immediate departure of Dr. Franklin, &ca.

This express was ordered immediately on Mr. Boudinot's return, that Congress may be apprised, and have time to deliberate even before the commissioners announce themselves. I have written in the greatest hurry, and thrown a chaos of words together.

I have barely time to acknowledge the receipt of your letter of the 5th. Mr. Conway's conduct irritates but does not surprise me. The truth of the matter with respect to his resignation is, that he expected to have been solicited to remain in the service, and to have made a great bustle, and increased his importance.—As for fighting, I know by what I saw at German Town, that his stomach is not so keen set for it as he pretends;—but his friends, Gates and Mifflin, sacrificed him at a time when he least expected it. However, he has fairly undone himself, and will be treated with that contempt which he deserves. I shall take the liberty of communicating this matter to the general.

I must beg the favour of you to send by the earliest

opportunity, a copy of the last resolves of Congress relative to the exchange of prisoners, the 21st ult°. It has been mislaid here, and the person who had the care of it wishes to avoid the wound to his sensibility which w^d arise from having the matter applied for officially with an explanation.

God preserve you, my dear father.

JOHN LAURENS.

The Honble Henry Laurens, Esqr.,

President of Congress, York.

(Private).

HEAD QUARTERS, 9th June, 1778.

My Dear Father :

I have received your kind favour of the 7th inst. accompanied by letters from Harry, and one from my wife. The former I send for your perusal; the latter contained nothing new.

Your letter to the general, and the copy of that to the commissioners Howe and Clinton, were dated May; but the mistake I apprehend in the original is of no consequence. I cannot forbear expressing my joy that Congress has replied with so much dignity to the first overtures made to them. If they pursue the conduct which they have marked out to themselves in their letter, they will act with propriety.

The insolence and infatuation of the British minister in sending commissioners to treat with America, under the act of Parliament which he pretends to call conciliatory, are without parallel.

I hope Congress will not even suffer the secretary of the commission to wait upon them, nor do any thing that looks like listening to their proposals. Mʳ Boudinot, who returned this evening from conference with the British commissary of prisoners, informs us that the preparations for evacuating still continue, and that it is impossible for the enemy to remain much longer. He says he has reason to think that they will not march through the Jerseys, but proceed to a convenient place down the Delaware on the Jersey side, and there embark. This opinion has been suggested before, and seems to be favoured by a contradiction of a report which prevailed some time ago of the enemy's collecting boats in Princes bay.

To-morrow the army will move to a camp about a mile in front of their present position. The unwholesome exhalations from the ground which we occupy has made this measure necessary. We shall be at hand to take possession of our field of battle, in case of any forward move on the part of the enemy. And while we are condemned to inactivity, we shall not swallow the effluvia arising from a deposit of various carcases and filth accumulated during six months.

I am much concerned that you are afflicted with any bodily pain. You do not mention what it is; I apprehend a return of your gout. Surely if ever a citizen deserved well of his country, you do; but your continued sacrifice of yourself will find its reward in the triumph of liberty.

God grant that your health of body may speedily be restored, and equal your health of mind.

Your most affectionate

JOHN LAURENS.

Doctor Ferguson, sec^y to the commission, was tutor to Ld Chesterfield at Geneva, where I became acquainted with him. He is a man known in the literary world, and whose profound knowledge makes him very respectable.

The Honble Henry Laurens, Esqr.,

President of Congress, York.

(Private).

HEAD QUARTERS, 11*th June*, 1778.

My Dear Father:

I enclose you a packet which I received from Philadelphia yesterday. You will be so good as to forward those letters which Mr. Manning commits to my care. The two letters which I have kept out of the bundle are one from Mr. Laurens, containing nothing new, and one for Anthony Butler, Esq., D. Q. M. G., which Gov. Johnston desires me to take charge of.

The commissioners ventured out yesterday as far as German Town with an escort of light troops, which with the number that have crossed into the Jerseys, left only 800 men in the city according to the account of a very intelligent deserter. Every account confirms the opinion that Sr H. Clinton is throwing his men over the Delaware by degrees, and that the remainder are constantly under marching orders.

The grenadiers have crossed the river, and the Anspachers have embarked.

The packet addressed to yourself and Congress, you will observe is sealed with the fond picture of a mother caressing her children. I am of opinion that the commissioners hope to do more by addressing themselves to individuals than public bodies. But what prospect can they have of succeeding in the least of their views. They must, I think, retire disgracefully, for I am persuaded that Congress will not lose sight of those well chosen land-marks which they declare they mean to steer by. The honour and interest of the nation, and the sacred regard which is due to treaties, unite to make us reject their overtures. From their conduct, one would think that they have as little opinion of our virtue and understanding, as they formerly had of our courage. It is our duty to convince them how much we have been calumniated in every respect, and to render their superior subtilty in negociations of as little avail as their greater experience in the art of war. I begin to regard Johnston as an apostate to the cause of liberty, and to place him among the number of those whose

secret wish is rather a change of men than measures.
The nominating him as a commissioner, and vesting
him and his colleagues with a power of making go-
vernors, are strokes of artful policy, against which
we cannot be too much on our guard.   His reputation
as a friend to America, his patriotic speeches in the
House of Commons, will be made the themes of
many a letter and discourse for seducing incautious
citizens.

God preserve you, my dear father.

JOHN LAURENS.

The Honble Henry Laurens, Esqr.,

  President of Congress, York.

(Private).

HEAD QUARTERS, 14th June, 1778.

My Dear Father:

I have barely a moment to thank you for your kind
favour of the 11th.

Congress, I am persuaded, will act with the dignity
and virtue which ought to characterize republicans,
in their answers to the British commissioners.   The
inquiry into the conduct of the late quarter masters,
must give pleasure to every man who wishes to see
the betrayers of public trusts brought to condign
punishment.

24

A party of the enemy were out yesterday, and in returning left a Mr Welford formerly surgeon in their service. This gentleman made himself disagreeable to the British officers, by his humanity to our wounded, and was obliged to resign. He has taken an opportunity of becoming a willing prisoner to a people whose sentiments are congenial to his own. This, I suppose in delicacy to him, must be kept a secret. Capt. McLane, an active, enterprising officer, who is constantly near the enemy's lines, sent him as a prisoner, and he must be announced as such. He quartered with General Lee last night, so that I had no opportunity of speaking to him; it is probable he may furnish us with a great deal of good intelligence.

I intend to write to you upon the subject of reforming our regiments, as the French call it. The weak, pitiful state of a great many of them, the little prospect of having them completed, the vast good that would result from purging the army of a number of officers, who besides are not unwilling to quit the service; in a word, the facility of bringing about a change which w^d be attended with more advantages than I have time to enumerate and develope, invites us irresistably to it.

I pray God to continue his blessings to you.

JOHN LAURENS.

The Baron de Steuben desires to be remembered to you. Some jealousies against him have occasioned

him great trouble, and interrupted his progress in the
military instruction.

The Honble Henry Laurens, Esqr.,

    York Town.

     HEAD QUARTERS, 15*th June*, 1778.

My Dear Father:

The world looks with anxious expectation for the
answer of Congress to the British commissioners.
A paper was said to have been pasted up in camp,
which contained the terms that are offered on their
part.   The general has given orders to have the
matter immediately traced.   Low artifices of this
kind discover feeble hopes of succeeding in a more
regular and open way.

Doctor Welford dined with us yesterday, but I had
no opportunity of conversing with him but in a pro-
miscuous way.   He confirms our opinion of the enemy's intention to pass through the Jerseys; says that
they have destroyed a vast number of blankets, etc.,
that they have strengthened their cavalry by mounting
many of their light infantry, or at least providing
horses, on which they are to be mounted occasionally.
By this means they will have, he thinks, 2,500 horsemen; that General Grant has escaped a court martial
for his conduct on the affair of Marquis de Lafayette,
by his powerful interest, but that he is much blamed

and abused in circles of officers. The doctor contradicts the report of Gov. Johnston's having been mobbed. He says, on the contrary, he is more respected than either of his colleagues, being regarded as the only proper person to gain the confidence of America, and succeed in the important business which they have in view.

Gov. Johnston, it is said, accuses Howe of having acted the part both of a villain and a fool;—the latter, in his military operations, the former in wanton and unauthorized destruction of private property.[1]

I hope the answer of Congress will arrive to-day, that it will be consistent with the reply already made to Gen¹ Clinton, &c., and if possible be calculated to give them less hopes.

The Baron de Steuben has received a letter from Mr de Beaumarchais, which informs him that war is rekindled between the Russians and Turks—that the king of Prussia is in Bohemia, at the head of 60,000 men, where he has already seized a fortified castle and two regiments, to show that he is determined to have satisfaction for the dismemberment of the electorate of Bavaria.

Gen¹ Reed has some very interesting gazettes, and a number or two of the *Parliamentary Register*, parts of which ought to be made public, without delay, in the course of calling for authentic papers, and

---

[1] Dr. Welford says so.

letters relative to American transactions. The minority has made some discoveries, which if they were generally known here, would prove an excellent antidote to the deceitful arts which the commissioners are now practising. A letter from Lord Howe and his brother, in Novem., 1776 (at a time when they thought nothing could turn the current of success from them), inclosed their proclamation offering a general pardon to the Americans. But they remark to the ministry that it will be proper to make a few examples, and upon the whole plainly indicate their intention to make as many as shall be found convenient, notwithstanding their promises.

You will receive by this courier an application from the captain of the General's guard. He has had the mortification of seeing himself outstripped by a vast number of his juniors who had no greater merit than himself. He has always done his duty in his station, and from what I saw of his behaviour at Barren Hill, wants only an opportunity to establish his character as an officer of bravery and steadiness, in action; and I really think he is entitled to a majority, at least to a brevet for one.

Adieu, my dear father; we pass a most tiresome time of inactivity and suspense in camp. I suppose you sympathize with us in the latter. I omitted to inform you above that Doctor Welford says the people in town have no other than salt provisions. Even that is brought to them from their vessels. As M^r W.

ought to pass for a prisoner of war, I do not mention his name as author of any intelligence, but in confidence to you, not that I think his history will be kept secret, but because I would not be the occasion of discovering it. As this courier was setting out hastily on a case of life and death, I did not intend to have said any thing on the subject of a reform, but as he delays I will venture to offer a few arguments in favour of it. Our regiments, as you well know, are many of them in a very weak state, and there is no kind of parity between them, which is the occasion of great trouble and confusion in encamping, marching, the detail for guards and detachments, &ca. To remedy these inconveniences, the General has issued an order to each brigadier to form his brigade into batallions of not less than 80 files, nor more than 111; by which means they will be sufficiently equalized to admit of their being regarded as a common measure for the army, and to facilitate the service. But as this is only a temporary arrangement, the field officers who are appointed by seniority to the command of these batallions, will not pay that attention to the welfare and discipline of the men under their command, which they would do in the case of their own soldiers; and, from an idea that there is no permanent relation between them, will not have that affection for them which the good of the service requires.

Had we any prospect that the States would furnish

their due quotas for completing their respective batallions, a reduction of regiments would be unnecessary; but as you and I very well know we have no
right to expect them to do their duty in this respect.

My letter is called for, and I must abruptly bid
adieu.

JOHN LAURENS.

HEAD QUARTERS, 16th June, 1778.

My Dear Father:

The Chevalier de Cambray informs me that he sets
out for York; I must write precipitately to have my
letter conveyed by him.

The state of intelligence yesterday was as follows:
That the baggage of the commissioners was packed
up, their linnen ordered from the washerwomen
finished or unfinished; the troops in town were the
third brigade which is composed of the Highlanders
and two British regiments, a few Hessians, the grenadiers and light infantry, and the cavalry; all the
vessels on the stocks had been burnt; some few
houses had been maliciously fired at the same time;
the park of artillery was reduced to five field pieces
and two howitzers; the horse tenders were at the
wharves with slings, &ca., in readiness; the Vigilant
and a few row galleys lay at the upper end of the
town to cover the passage of the troops; the commissary of the light horse had put all his baggage in his

waggon; orders had been given to the 3ᵈ brigade to be
in readiness for marching this morning at 2 o'clock.
This intelligence was given by a very faithful fellow
whose mother washed for the commissioners, and
who on former occasions has given us accurate and
useful intelligence. This day, three deserters, one
of them from the corps of grenadiers, confirmed many
of the foregoing circumstances. A letter from Capᵗ
McLane, dated at noon, informs me that all the
enemy's park had crossed the river; that the Highlanders were then crossing; that he had marched
towards the enemy's redoubts, caused several of them
to be manned, and exchanged a few shot with a
party that advanced in front of them. It is his
opinion as well as that of others, that the city will be
completely evacuated to-morrow.

The prevailing opinion is, that one division of the
army will march by way of Trenton, and another by
a lower road, in marching through the Jersies.

An account dated yesterday from the city says that
the enemy have taken all the horses they could possibly collect; logs, planks, blocks, &c., have been
swept to form such magazines as they probably may
want in the West Indies.

My dearest friend, you will excuse this letter which
has been written as fast as ever my hand could
conduct my pen, and believe me ever your most
affectionate

JOHN LAURENS.

Inclosed is a letter which Mr Morris desires may be forwarded to its address.

M^r De Cottineau has presented the General with a very elegant plumage set in gold, with this celebrated address of Henry the 4th of France to his soldiers engraved on it:

Ne perdez pas de vue mon Panache blanc; vous le trouverez toujours au Chemin de l'honeur et de la victoire.

Don't lose sight of my white plumage, you will ever find it in the road which leads to honour and victory.

HEAD QUARTERS, ENGLISH TOWN, 30*th June*, 1778.

My Dear Father:

I was exceedingly chagrined that public business prevented my writing to you from the field of battle, when the General sent his dispatches to Congress. The delay, however, will be attended with this advantage, that I shall be better able to give you an account of the enemy's loss; tho' I must now content myself with a very succinct relation of this affair. The situation of the two armies on Sunday was as follows: Genl Washington, with the main body of our army, was at 4 miles distance from English Town. Genl Lee, with a chosen advanced corps, was *at* that town. The enemy were retreating down the road which leads to Middle Town; their flying army composed

25

(as it was said), of 2 batallions of British grenadiers, 1 Hessian grend^{rs}, 1 batallion of light infantry, 1 regiment of guards, 2 brigades of foot, 1 reg^t of dragoons and a number of mounted and dismounted Jagers. The enemy's rear was preparing to leave Monmouth village, which is 6 miles from this place, when our advanced corps was marching towards them. The militia of the country kept up a random running fire with the Hessian Jagers; no mischief was done on either side. I was with a small party of horse, reconnoitering the enemy, in an open space before Monmouth, when I perceived two parties of the enemy advancing by files in the woods on our right and left, with a view, as I imagined, of enveloping our small party, or preparing a way for a skirmish of their horse. I immediately wrote an account of what I had seen to the General, and expressed my anxiety on account of the languid appearance of the Continental troops under Genl Lee.

Some person in the mean time reported to Genl Lee that the enemy were advancing upon us in two columns, and I was informed that he had, in consequence, ordered Varnum's brigade, which was in front, to repass a bridge which it had passed. I went myself, and assured him of the real state of the case; his reply to me was, that his accounts had been so contradictory, that he was utterly at a loss what part to take. I repeated my account to him in positive distinct terms, and returned to make farther discoveries.

I found that the two parties had been withdrawn from the wood, and that the enemy were preparing to leave Monmouth. I wrote a second time to Gen[l] Washington. Gen[l] Lee at length gave orders to advance. The enemy were forming themselves on the Middle Town road, with their light infantry in front, and cavalry on the left flank, while a scattering, distant fire was commenced between our flanking parties and theirs. I was impatient and uneasy at seeing that no disposition was made, and endeavoured to find out Gen[l] Lee to inform him of what was doing, and know what was his disposition. He told me that he was going to order some troops to march below the enemy and cut off their retreat. Two pieces of artillery were posted on our right without a single foot soldier to support them. Our men were formed piecemeal in front of the enemy, and there appeared to be no general plan or disposition calculated on that of the enemy; the nature of the ground, or any of the other principles which generally govern in these cases.

The enemy began a cannonade from two parts of their line; their whole body of horse made a furious charge upon a small party of our cavalry and dissipated them, and drove them till the appearance of our infantry, and a judicious discharge or two of artillery made them retire precipitately. Three regiments of ours that had advanced in a plain open country towards the enemy's left flank, were ordered by Gen[l] Lee to retire and occupy the village of Monmouth. They were no sooner formed there, than they were ordered to quit that post and gain the woods. One order succeeded another with a rapidity and indecision calculated to ruin us. The enemy had changed their front and were advancing in full march towards us; our men were fatigued with the excessive heat. The artillery horses were not in condition to make a brisk retreat. A new position was ordered, but not generally communicated, for part of the troops were forming on the right of the ground, while others were marching away, and all the artillery driving off. The enemy, after a short halt, resumed their pursuit; no cannon was left to check their progress. A regiment was ordered to form behind a fence, and as speedily commanded to retire. All this disgraceful retreating, passed without the firing of a musket, over ground which might have been disputed inch by inch. We passed a defile and arrived at an eminence beyond, which was defended on one hand by an impracticable fen, on the other by thick woods where our men would have fought to advantage. Here, fortunately for the honour of the army, and the welfare of America, Gen¹ Washington met the troops retreating in disorder, and without any plan to make an opposition. He ordered some pieces of artillery to be brought up to defend the pass, and some troops to form and defend the pieces. The artillery was too distant to be brought up readily, so that there was but little opposition given here. A few shot though, and a little skirmishing in the wood checked the enemy's career. The Gen¹ expressed his astonishment at this unaccountable retreat. Mʳ Lee indecently replied that the attack was contrary to his advice and opinion in council. We were obliged to retire to a position, which, though hastily reconnoitered, proved an excellent one. Two regiments were formed behind a fence in front of the position. The enemy's horse advanced in full charge with admirable bravery to the distance of forty paces, when a general discharge from these two regiments did great execution among them, and made them fly with the greatest precipitation. The grenadiers succeeded to the attack. At this time my horse was killed under me. In this spot the action was hottest, and there was considerable slaughter of British grenadiers. The General ordered Woodford's brigade with some artillery to take possession of an eminence on the enemy's left, and cannonade from thence. This produced an excellent effect. The enemy were prevented from advancing on us, and confined themselves to cannonade with a show of turning our left flank. Our artillery answered theirs with the greatest vigour. The General seeing that our left flank was secure, as the ground was open and commanded by it, so that the enemy could not attempt to turn it without exposing their own flank to a heavy fire from our artillery, and causing to pass in review before us, the force employed for turning us. In the mean time, Gen¹ Lee continued retreating. Baron Steuben was order'd to form the broken troops in the rear. The cannonade was incessant and the General ordered parties to advance from time to time and engage the British grenadiers and guards. The horse shewed themselves no more. The grenadiers showed their backs and retreated every where with precipitation. They returned, however, again to the charge, and were again repulsed. They finally retreated and got over the strong pass, where, as I mentioned before, Gen[l] Washington first rallied the troops. We advanced in force and continued masters of the ground; the standards of liberty were planted in triumph on the field of battle. We remained looking at each other, with the defile between us, till dark, and they stole off in silence at midnight. We have buried of the enemy's slain, 233, principally grenadiers; forty odd of their wounded whom they left at Monmouth, fell into our hands. Several officers are our prisoners. Among their killed are Co[l] Moncton, a captain of the guards, and several captains of grenadiers. We have taken but a very inconsiderable number of prisoners, for want of a good body of horse. Deserters are coming in as usual. Our officers and men behaved with that bravery which becomes freemen, and have convinced the world that they can beat British grenadiers. To name any one in particular w[d] be a kind of injustice to the rest. There are some, however, who came more immediately under my view, whom

I will mention that you may know them. B. Genl Wayne, Col. Barber, Col. Stewart, Col. Livingston, Col. Oswald of the artillery, Capt Doughty deserve well of their country, and distinguished themselves nobly.

The enemy buried many of their dead that are not accounted for above, and carried off a great number of wounded. I have written diffusely, and yet I have not told you all. Genl Lee, I think, must be tried for misconduct. However, as this is a matter not generally known, tho' it seems almost universally wished for, I would beg you, my dear father, to say nothing of it.

You will oblige me much by excusing me to Mr Drayton for not writing to him. I congratulate you, my dear father, upon this seasonable victory, and am ever

Your most dutiful and affectionate

JOHN LAURENS.

The Honble Henry Laurens, Esqr.

We have no returns of our loss as yet. The proportion on the field of battle appeared but small. We have many good officers wounded.

HEAD QUARTERS (on the lovely banks of the Raritan,
            opposite New Brunswick), 2d *July*, 1778.

My Dear Father:

I had the pleasure of writing to you the day before
yesterday, from English Town, but through some
mistake my letter was not delivered to the express,
altho it was written in a hurry. I recollect no circumstance in it relative to our late engagement,
which farther inquiry and consideration do not confirm. From a second view of the ground, as well as
the accounts I have since had of the enemy's strength
and designs, it is evident to me that Mr Clinton's
whole flying army would have fallen into our hands,
but for a defect of abilities or good will in the commanding officer of our advanced corps. His precipi-
tate retreat spread a baneful influence every where.
The most sanguine hope scarcely extended farther,
when the Commander in chief rallied his troops, than
to an orderly retreat; but by his intrepidity and presence of mind, a firm line of troops was formed on a
good position, from whence he cannonaded with
advantage, and detached light parties in front, who
drove the enemy from the field. Genl Clinton and
Lord Cornwallis were both present at the action.

The reason for not pursuing them farther with the
main body of our army was, that people well acquainted with the country said that the strength of
the ground would render it impracticable for us to

injure them essentially; and that the sandy, parched soil, together with the heat of the sun, would probably occasion us considerable loss. From the specimen of yesterday's march we have reason to think it fortunate that we took the part we have done; the heat of the weather, thirsty soil, and heavy sand, reduced us to the necessity of bringing on many of our weaker men in waggons.

We are now arrived in a delightful country where we shall halt and refresh ourselves. Bathing in the Raritan, and the good living of the country will speedily refresh us. I wish, my dear father, that you could ride along the banks of this delightful river. Your zeal for the public service will not at this time permit it. But the inward satisfaction which you must feel from a patriotic discharge of your duty, is infinitely superior to the delights of retirement and ease. I admire your constant virtue, and will imitate your example.

Your most affectionate
JOHN LAURENS.

Col. Morgan writes this day, that the rear of the enemy is a mile below Middle Town; that he has had a skirmish with several of their light parties, which has cost them some lives. He had only one man wounded. Desertions continue, and I suppose will be very considerable at the moment of embarkation.

I have seen the General much embarrassed this day, on the subject of those who distinguished themselves in the battle of Monmouth. To name a few, and be silent with regard to many of equal-merit w^d be an injustice to the latter; to pass the whole over unnoticed w^d be an unpardonable slight; indiscriminate praise of the whole w^d be an unfair distribution of rewards; and yet, when men generally conducted themselves so well as our officers did, this matter is allowable and is eligible, because least liable to give offence.

The merit of restoring the day, is due to the General; and his conduct was such throughout the affair as has greatly increased my love and esteem for him. My three brother aids gained themselves great applause by their activity and bravery, while the three secretaries acted as military men on this occasion, and proved themselves as worthy to wield the sword as the pen.

Genl Steuben, his aids and your son, narrowly escaped being surrounded by the British horse, early on the morning of the action. We reconnoitered them rather too nearly, and Ld Cornwallis sent the dragoons of his guard to make us prisoners. Genl Clinton saw [1] the Baron's star, and the whole pursuit

---

[1] A dragoon deserter from the enemy just informs us of this. He says three others came off with him, and that the Hessians are deserting amazingly.

was directed at him; but we all escaped, the dragoons fearing an ambuscade of infantry.

We have buried Col. Moncton with the honours of war.

The Honble Henry Laurens, Esqr.,
    President of Congress, Philadelphia.
    (Private).

HEAD QUARTERS NEAR BRUNSWICK, *6th July*, 1778.
My Dear Father :

I beg leave to introduce to your acquaintance, and recommend to your civilities the Marquis de la Vienne. He arrived in camp while we were at Valley Forge, with recommendatory letters to the Marquis de Lafayette, and has been with him ever since. He is now going to present himself to Congress. If he asks for any thing, they will best know whether his request is reasonable and well founded. Unfortunately there is a prejudice against foreigners in many of our officers. It is not without uneasiness that some of them see Baron de Steuben, who has certainly rendered us very important services, and who is without doubt as capable of commanding as any major general we have, appointed to the temporary command of a division in the absence of so many major generals.

The last accounts from the enemy are, that they

were busily employed in embarking their baggage and horses. Yesterday I had a view of their fleet, which appeared to be getting under weigh.

Six grenadiers came in yesterday, one of them a very intelligent fellow, says that desertion prevails so much among them that unless they are speedily embarked, their army will dwindle into nothing.

I felicitate you, my dear father, upon the many happy events which have taken place during your presidency, and upon the happy prospects which continue to present themselves. May God preserve you to enjoy the complete triumph of liberty and your country.

Your most affectionate

JOHN LAURENS.

The Honble Henry Laurens, Esqr.,

President of Congress, Philadelphia.

Fav^d by the Marquis de la Vienne.

HEAD QUARTERS NEAR BRUNSWICK, 7th July, 1778.

My Dear Father:

We are just about to march. Seventy miles are between us and King's Ferry, where we shall probably cross the North river. The last intelligence from the enemy is, that they had passed the breach which the sea has made between Sandy Hook and the main, and had taken up their bridge after them. They were embarking with the greatest expedition. They left a number of waggons behind them, and cut the throats of a great many horses. Three signal guns were fired from the fleet the day before yesterday morning, and they appeared to be all under weigh yesterday.

Col. Morgan informs us that he had taken 30 prisoners, and received 100 deserters. I suppose he counts from the time of his having been detached. I wish I had leisure, and something more interesting to write to you, my dear father; but our rear has left the ground long since, and we must march.

Your most affectionate

JOHN LAURENS.

The Honble Henry Laurens, Esqr.,
 President of Congress, Philadelphia.
(Private).

HEAD QUARTERS, 13th July, 1778.

I have barely time, my dearest friend and father, to say that my heart overflows with gratitude at the repeated proofs of your tender love; and must defer answering your kind letters of the 6th and 10th, 'till my return from Count D'Estaing's fleet, where the General has thought proper to send me with dispatches. I must immediately prepare for my journey and voyage. I could wish that Monsr Le Comte were furnished with a proper number of intelligent coast pilots; that as many pilot boats, schooners and

other small swift sailing vessels were employed under
the conduct of judicious seamen, to reconnoitre the
enemy's fleet whenever it appears at sea, and give
the French admiral the earliest account of their
strength, &ca., as well as keep him constantly advised
afterwards of all their motions.

The movement of our army across the North river,
to make demonstration near N. York, may have a
happy effect in preventing the English admiral from
making his fleet so strong as he otherwise would.

God protect you, my dear father.

JOHN LAURENS.

The Honble Henry Laurens, Esqr.,
    President of Congress, Philadelphia.
(Private).

18th July, 1778.

My Dear Father:

I am very happy in having an opportunity of introducing to your acquaintance, General Forman, a
gentleman for whom I have the highest esteem, on
account of his indefatigability and great sacrifices in
the public service.

You will discover at a first interview that he is a
man of enlightened understanding, and will receive
much satisfaction from his account of the most interesting military transactions of the present day. I
must refer you to this gentleman, likewise for a more

minute relation of the obstacles which have delayed
the operations of the French fleet. We were on board
of the Admiral together, and he had an opportunity of
being acquainted with the difficulties with which the
Admiral has struggled.

Whatever civilities or services it may be in your
power to offer to Gen¹ Forman, will give particular
pleasure to

Your most affectionate

JOHN LAURENS.

The Honble Henry Laurens, Esqr.,

 President of Congress, Philadelphia.

I have barely time, paper and ink to write my dear
father a hurried official letter.

Upon my arrival here with dispatches from the
General to Admiral D'Estaing, I found that the
fleet laboured under the greatest difficulty in procuring water; its distance from the shore was too great
to roll the casks down to the place of embarcation;
the disaffected inhabitants either refused their waggons, or granted them only at an exorbitant price.
I have done every thing in my power to remedy this
evil: but as we cannot have too many resources, I
would propose that any fast sailing small craft in the
Delaware may be immediately employed in bringing
water round. The southerly winds which prevail on
the coast at this season, will give them a quick voy-

age, and they will be in time if they arrive with La Chimère.

It would give me pleasure to speak to you, particularly of the great qualities of the admiral. He has inspired me in the short acquaintance I have had with him, with uncommon respect. He laments the insipid part he is playing—keeping the English fleet blocked up within Sandy Hook; and taking prizes within their view every day does not satisfy a man of his great ideas. When six prizes were brought into him yesterday, he desired the major of the fleet to give some directions about those *Drugs*, and sighed at not being engaged in a way in which more honour was to be acquired.

Two of the prizes that have been taken since my being here were armed, one with 4 and the other with 10 guns. One had a quantity of specie on board—the profits of prizes taken from us. The fleet, men and officers appear to be in fine health, and eager to distinguish themselves in a naval combat. As much as it is against my desire, I must break off, an express rider must be diligent.

My dearest friend and father, I pray God to protect you.

JOHN LAURENS.

Black Point, 18th July, 1778.

HEAD QUARTERS, 22*d July*, 1778.

My Dear Father:

Permit me to introduce to your acquaintance the Baron D'Arendt, Col. of the German batallion, who in consequence of disputes with his corps of officers, which he thinks make it inconvenient with his honour to serve with them again, and from the improbability of his being placed elsewhere in an agreeable military station, has determined to resign his commission, and goes to Congress to obtain their leave. I have received both entertainment and improvement in conversing with him as a military man, and will be obliged to you to shew him such civilities as your leisure and your public business will allow.

I am, with the most tender attachment and respect,

Your dutiful son

JOHN LAURENS.

The Honble Henry Laurens, Esqr.,

President of Congress, Philadelphia.

PROVIDENCE, *4th August*, 1778.

I thank you, my dearest friend and father, for your tender letter of the 26th ult°. I was upon the point of writing to you the 22^d, when I was ordered to fly with important dispatches to Govr Trumbull, General Sullivan and the Count D'Estaing. I commissioned

27

one of my friends to acquaint you of the circumstance; but perhaps the multiplicity of affairs in which I left him involved will have made him lose sight of the matter. In 48 hours over the worst, and in some parts the most obscure road that I ever travel'd, I arrived at Providence, had a conference with Gen¹ Sullivan, and proceeded immediately with pilots provided for the French fleet, down to Point Judith. Boats were soon provided and everything put in readiness for boarding the Admiral as soon as he should announce himself by the firing of five cannon. Here I waited in a very disagreeable kind of company 'till the morning of the 29th, for tho' the squadron anchored off Block island the preceding afternoon, the haziness of the weather rendered them invisible to us. In the morning when the fog was dissipated, their appearance was as sudden as a change of decorations in an opera house. Upon my delivering Gen¹ Washington's dispatches, and Gen¹ Sullivan's containing a plan of operations, the Admiral informed me his intention had been to proceed immediately into the main channel of Newport and attack the enemy's batteries. The day, however, began to be too far spent. It was expedient to distribute intelligent pilots in the squadron, and, in pursuance of Gen¹ Sullivan's plan, the main channel was blocked up with the squadron. A ship of the line was ordered up the west channel, and two frigates and a tender up the east. By consulting the map, you will find that there are three

entrances to Rhode Island ; one on the east of Rhode
Island between it and the main, called the Seakonnet
passage ; one on the west, between it and Cononicut
island, which is the principal or main passage; a third
between Cononicut and the main land, commonly
called the western passage.   In the first Gen¹ Sullivan
informed the Admiral there were two galleys and one
small frigate; in the second, two frigates besides two
galleys, and two or three frigates at Newport; in the
last, two small frigates ; farther, that he estimated the
enemy's land force, including three regiments posted
on Cononicut at 7,000 effective.

General Sullivan's plan founded on these data, was
that the Admiral should detach a proper force up the
eastern and western channels, to take the enemy's
ships stationed in each; to block up the main channel
with the remainder of the squadron, so as effectually
to cut off the retreat of their ships, and to prevent the
arrival of reinforcements.   The French ships in the
eastern and western channels were afterwards to cover
the passage of the American troops from Tiverton and
Bristol.   The troops were not to amuse themselves
with attacking the works in the northern part of the
island; but a sufficient detachment was to be left to
be a guard upon the troops posted in those works,
while the main body was to advance rapidly to the
attack of the fort and redoubts, which immediately
environ the town of Newport.   At the moment of
that attack the count was to force the passage into

Newport harbour, silence the enemy's batteries, cannonade the town, and disembark his marines and land forces at the most proper place for seconding the American attack.

The Sagittaire, a ship of the line, went up the western passage on the morning of the 30th, and was fired upon by a two gun battery of 24 pounders, which the enemy had on the west side of Cononicut. The Sagittaire returned a broadside as she passed, and we discovered from the Admiral's ship an explosion at the battery, which induced us to believe that the enemy had abandoned it.

The ship received two scratches in her hull, and proceeded to her station.

The Aimable and Alemene frigates accompanied by the Stanley (prize) tender, went up the eastern passage. Upon their approach, the enemy set fire to the Kingfisher 20 gun sloop, and to the Lamb galley mounting —— and sent the Spitfire galley mounting —— in form of a fire ship. The Count de Grace commanded the boat which was ordered to tow the latter off. She blew up soon after the grapnel was fixed, and the gallant officer with his crew escaped unhurt. An officer who went on board with a party to extinguish the flames of the Kingfisher, had an escape equally providential. Her powder room blew up while they were on board, and they received no injury. The hull drifted over to the main and her guns will be saved.

From the enemy's keeping possession of the island of Cononicut, the admiral concluded that it was an important post to them. The battery which they had on the east side of it, afforded a cross fire upon the entrance of the harbour, and the three regiments there made it an object. The count therefore thought it expedient that we should make ourselves masters of it. The most effectual way of attacking it would have been by disembarking troops on the west side of it, and sending a proper force of ships up the main channel to run through the fire of the batteries at the entrance, and take a proper position for cutting off the communication between Rhode Island and Cononicut, so as to prevent the enemy's throwing across reinforcements; but, upon inquiry, it was found impracticable to anchor the ships any where out of the reach of the enemy's batteries, so that after running the gauntlet at the entrance, the ships w^d have been exposed to a constant deliberate fire in the harbour. These difficulties obliged the count to renounce the plan of sending ships up the main channel for this duty. It was then inquired whether the ships might not effect the business by going up the western channel, turning the north point of Cononicut and coming down the main channel. By this means they would in the first instance avoid the cross fire at the entrance, and might take such a position relatively to the harbour as w^d discourage the enemy from throwing across succours. But the most experienced pilots

informed us that to effect this detour, the ships must
either have a wind which w^d answer equally for going
up the western and coming down the main channel,
or, that after going up with a fair wind, they would
be obliged to beat down the main channel, or, lastly,
they would be obliged to wait for a fair wind to bring
them down from the north end of Cononicut. The
delay and uncertainty incident to the first and last
put them out of the question. The second was pronounced impracticable on account of the narrowness
of the main channel above Newport, which w^d not
allow scope enough for the ships work^g, and missing
stays w^d be fatal in such circumstances.

It was determined therefore, that in order to gain
Cononicut, a body of militia sh^d be applied for to
make us equal to such a reinforcement as we thought
the enemy could spare. Col. Fleury and myself went
by the admiral's desire, to make application for this
purpose. In our way we learnt that some American
privateers had been on the island, and that the enemy
had evacuated the battery which fired on the Sagittaire. We met Genl Sullivan on his way to the fleet,
where he was going to have a conference with the
Admiral, and propose some changes in his plan. He
was received on board with the guard of marines,
and the drums beating to arms; and, at his departure,
the ship was manned and fifteen cannon fired.

The evening of the 30th, the outermost ships made
signals of the appearance of a fleet. The Admiral got

his squadron in readiness for fight and chase; but the fleet put about and escaped under the veil of night. It proved to be 8 transports with wood from Long Island bound to Newport, and conveyed by a frigate.

On the evening of the 31ˢᵗ, the Admiral sent a party to reconnoitre Cononicut, and discover whether the enemy had really abandoned all their batteries as was reported. It was found that they had.

The next morning the Admiral landed in order to view the enemy's batteries from the east side of Cononicut. We found in the battery which fired on the Sagittaire two 24 pounders spiked, and all their heavy ammunition. From the battery on the E. end, we had a distinct view of the town shipping, and batteries. The latter lost that respectability which they had on paper; the fire from the ships of the line must annihilate them in an hour. The fort on an eminence called Domine Hill, back of the town, may require our heavy artillery and some shells. We have every reason to believe that we shall effect our landing on the island without opposition, as the enemy seemed to have concentrated their force in Newport.

The admiral has disembarrassed himself of his prisoners, sick and prizes. He is in perfect readiness for acting his part, and as anxious as a man can be.

General Sullivan has exerted himself to the utmost, but the backwardness of the militia called for from the neighboring states the necessity of constructing transport boats to supply the place of those destroyed by the enemy in their last descent, and many other necessary preparations which require time, have delayed us till now, and I find it impossible to tell you with precision on what day we shall be ready.

I fear, my dearest father, that I have tired you with detail, and that from a habit of speaking of our operations with my finger on the map, I may in some places not have expressed my meaning fully enough, but my time unluckily will not permit to remove these inconveniences by writing a new letter. I am just come from the admiral to see if it will be possible by any means to hasten our land operations. The French squadron will want a great quantity of provisions whether they winter here or return to France. No biscuit is to be had here. Pennsylvania must furnish flour, and bakers should be employed there immediately.

It is reported that 20 sail of Spanish ships are on the coast. Pray, who is Don Juan de Miralles?

I am ever your most affectionate

JOHN LAURENS.

In the letter which I wrote you from Black point, I mentioned the Admiral's intention to send his prisoners to Philadelphia. Some difficulties induced him to change his plan; they are all landed here.

Deserters from Rhode Island say the troops are in want of provisions, and look upon themselves as prisoners.

The Marquis de Lafayette, with a division from the grand army, is arrived, and his men have had time to refresh themselves. Gen[l] Greene is likewise arrived.

Gen[l] Sullivan's 1st estimate of the enemy's land force is too high; they cannot have above 5,000 men, and the Gen[l] begins to think so himself.

The Honble Henry Laurens,
　　　President of Congress.

My Dear Father:

I have just had the satisfaction of receiving your kind letter of the 13th. The relation of what has passed, since I last had the pleasure of writing, will not in general amuse you, but it is necessary that you sh[d] know it, and I will be exceedingly brief. According to the first plan proposed by General Sullivan, the American forces were to land on the east side of Rhode Island under cover of the fire of three frigates stationed in the eastern channel for that purpose. A signal was to be given immediately as our boats should begin to cross, and another when the descent should be effected. Upon the latter, the French troops were to disembark on the east side of the island, and a junction was to be formed as speedily as possible; but the ambition of an individual and national pride discovered insuperable obstacles to this disposition. The Marquis de Lafayette aspired to the command of the French troops in conjunction with

28

the flower of Gen[l] Sullivan's army.   In a visit which he
had paid to the fleet, he prevailed upon the Count
D'Estaing to write upon this subject.   The count inti-
mated in his letter a desire that some good American
troops sh[d] be annexed to the French, adding that if
the command of them were given to M. de Lafayette
it w[d] be a means of facilitating the junction between
the troops of the two nations, as he was acquainted
with the service of both, and that in case any naval
operations sh[d] require his (the count's) return on board
the squadron, the Marquis w[d] naturally take the
command in his absence which w[d] prevent many
difficulties that w[d] arise on that account.   The
Marquis strenuously contended that a considerable
detachment of select troops ought to be annexed to
the French.   The pride of his nation would never
suffer the present disposition to take place, as by it
the French batallions w[d] land under cover of the
American fire, and play a humiliating secondary part.

The arguments against gratifying him in his request
were these : General Sullivan's army contained a
very small proportion of regular troops ; it was necessary that a main body capable of resisting the enemy's
force should exist, as a contrary conduct w[d] expose
either division to a total defeat or a vigorous attack
from the enemy.   The Marquis, however, seemed
much dissatisfied, and his private views withdrew
his attention wholly from the general interest.

On the 8th Gen[l] Sullivan received a letter from the

Admiral, in which he says that the disposition for disembarking is militarily impossible. That the American generals were now for the first time furnished with an opportunity of discovering the value which they set on the French alliance, by the number and composition of the troops which they w^d annex to the French. It was not for him to point out the number, but he w^d gladly have it in his power to give an account both to the Congress and his king of the American detachm^t which should be sent to him. In consequence of this letter, it was determined that Jackson's regiment, and as many good militia as in the whole w^d amount to 1,000 men sh^d be sent under the command of the marquis. The tardiness of the militia and the impossibility of completing the transport boats so soon as expected, and the slow arrival of the heavy cannon, had obliged Genl Sullivan more than once to procrastinate the attack. He had fixed on the 9th, and for the reasons mentioned in my last, the Count was to force his passage with the squadron, on the 8th.

The Genl found it impossible to keep his word, and wrote to appoint another day on which he declared he w^d make his descent at all events.

The Count, however, had made his arrangements and entered the harbour on the 8th. A thundering cannonade was kept up between the batteries and ships as they passed. The injury to the latter is not worth notice.

9th, Gen[l] Sullivan received intelligence both from deserters and inhabitants, that the enemy had evacuated all their redoubts and batteries on the north part of the island. He took the hardy resolution of availing himself of this move and threw his whole army across.[1] This measure gave much umbrage to the French officers. They conceived their troops injured by our landing first, and talked like women disputing precedence in a country dance, instead of men engaged in pursuing the common interest of two great nations.

Admiral Howe's fleet appeared in the offing.

10th. The French squadron passed the batteries of Newport (receiving their fire and returning broadsides), without receiving any damage by reason of the distance, and gave chase to the British fleet. On the 11th such a storm of wind and rain arose as filled us with anxiety for the French squadron. The army suffered much during the bad weather for want of tents, and on account of the impossibility of crossing the ferry, which circumstance reduced our magazines to a low ebb.

On the 15th, the army moved to a position for commencing its operations against the enemy, and some works were thrown up the same night for its security.

On the evening of the 16th, a battery of protection and its communication were begun. The next morn-

---

[1] An officer was sent immediately to give the Admiral notice of it.

ing as soon as our unfinished work could be discovered, the enemy's batteries began to fire on it.   Our
works have been carrying on every night since; and
as long as day-light lasts there is generally a slow
firing kept up on each side, without any effect worth
mentioning.   On account of the great distance, the
method that has been hitherto pursued will prove very
tedious if continued.

20th. The French squadron appears and terminates
much anxiety.   The Admiral's ship and the Marseilles
were dismasted in the storm.   The former totally dismasted, without a rudder, was attacked by a British
fifty gun ship, which she obliged to sheer off, by
bringing her stern chasers to bear.   Imagine the cruel
situation of the Count to see his ship thus insulted,
after having arrived in the midst of the English
squadron and preparing for a combat in which victory
was inevitably his; but a most dreadful storm of
which he had no idea, dispersed every thing.

I was going on, but was called away upon the most
important business.

The council of war on board the French vessels
have determined that the squadron ought to go immediately to Boston to refit.   I am going on board with
a solemn protest against it.

Adieu.

JOHN LAURENS.

22 *Aug*[t], 1778.

HEAD QUARTERS, 15th Septem., 1778.

My Dear Father:

I avail myself of Col. Bannister's offer to have the pleasure of writing to you.

The intelligence which we have received since my last, confirms the idea of a grand move on the part of the enemy. A British matross who deserted the day before yesterday declares that he assisted in embarking artillery and stores, and says that five thousand troops are destined for the West Indies. Accounts received some days since of taylors being employed in stripping regimental coats of their lining and making up thin overalls and waistcoats, indicates an expedition to a warmer climate than any on the territories of the United States, in the approaching season. It is reported that many merchants are disposing of their wares by vendue at low rates. I am not acquainted with the persons to whom we are indebted for intelligence, and therefore cannot be sure whether they are the dupes of reports circulated by the enemy, or give us a relation of facts that may be depended on.

There appears to be no other object here for the enemy but the French squadron, nor elsewhere but the French islands. Either will require an exertion of their whole force, and the latter perhaps will upon several accounts be preferred.

Some people are of opinion that they will aim first at the ruin of the squadron, and then direct their

whole force against some French island. It is difficult to predict what measures will be pursued by
men, who have been so eccentric in their military
operations.

If they had been vigorous, the French squadron
might have fallen a sacrifice, and it would have been
a tottering stroke to the marine of France. But their
delay and the disposition which has been made by our
general, have, I hope, pretty well secured an object of
such importance to the common cause.

It is to be urged in excuse for them that Byron's
fleet suffered by a storm, and that the crews belonging
to it are in very bad health. The division of six ships
under Rear Admiral Parker at New York, has been
obliged to land five hundred, some say a thousand
men; besides, you know, two of his fleet (one of them
the Admiral's ship), are said to be missing, and one, to
have put back to Portsmouth.

The army will move from its present position to-
morrow morning.

God preserve you, my dear father.

JOHN LAURENS.

Mr. Galvan, an officer in one of our Carolina regiments brought me two letters of very particular
recommendation from the Bn. de Holzendorff and
Mr. Reid. Some of our family informed me that in
a letter to me, which I have not yet received, this person was mentioned in such a manner as excluded him

from favour. When he called upon me, therefore, I did not introduce him to the General; he found means however, to introduce himself, and ask the General's protection. The Gen¹ asked me in private whether this was not the person alluded to in your letter; I told him he was; the General then left the room without taking any farther notice of him. Galvan finding he had so little encouragement to stay, retired. Yesterday he came again and produced a letter which he said he intended to send to you, in which he desires that through my mediation he might be restored to your friendship, and desired leave to read it. I told him he was the master to write what he pleased, but that I should not confirm that in my letters to you. He asked me the reason of the cold reception the Gen¹ had given him. I told him that I must frankly inform him that we had all heard very serious matters to his disadvantage, and besides that, as his only object here was to serve as a volunteer, he might depend upon it, that there was no opening for him. He asked me whether I had received any letter from you respecting him; I told him I had not. He desired to have an opportunity of justifying himself before the General, but this I waived. I was then called off for some business, and he went away saying that he would call again.

His Excellency, Henry Laurens, Esqr.,

President of Congress, Philadelphia.

(Private).

HEAD QUARTERS, 24*th September*, 1778.

My Dear Father :

I have received your kind favour of the 17th inst.

The information which you give me relative to my hospitable acquaintance, gives me great pain. I had conceived an esteem for him, and it afflicts me to find a new instance of the depravity of my species.

I am sorry that Kinloch did not return to America sooner. His former sentiments on the present contest, give reason to suspect, if he is a convert, that success on our side has alone operated the change. Something may be drawn in palliation of his conduct from the education he received, and the powerful influence which his guardian had over him.

Beresford's circumstances were peculiar, he has been uniformly a friend to his country.

The approach of the period which you allude to, occasions the greatest anxiety in my mind. The public interest and my own lead me to wish that you may continue in the august assembly of the states. I dread your being so remote from where my duty places me, and see collected in one view all the painful consequences of it. It was my intention at all events to have paid you the homage of my love in Philadelphia, at the close of the present campaign. We are at present in a disagreeable state of suspense. Continued preparations in New York announce a very considerable embarkation. Our spies inform us that

29

a council of war had been held, and continued for
three days. Lord Howe has certainly arrived. Gen[l]
Gray's troops had returned by way of the sound and
been relanded. Admiral Byron in the Princess Royal
of 90 guns, accompanied by the Culloden, Cap[t] Bal-
four of 74, had arrived at New York, according to
the *Gazette* of that place; but I believe the truth was,
that they only arrived off the Hook. They are since
arrived at Newport where they are refitting. It is
probable that the Princess Royal could not get into
port at N. York, without taking out the greatest part
of her artillery. Accounts from various quarters inform us, that Lord Howe is preparing for England,
and that Admiral Byron will take the command.

The arrival of the August packet will in all probability determine his operations. The sickly state of
his crews, and the damage which his ships suffered in
the storm, have rendered him inactive here till the
opportunity is lost for the only enterprise which remains for the enemy's combined land and naval force
in America.

Nothing remains for them, but to render the
garrisons of Quebec and Halifax respectable (at
the latter place, the seventieth regiment, the Duke
of Hamilton's and the Duke of Argyle's highland
men, according to the N. York paper, have arrived),
to evacuate New York and Rhode Island, and
withdraw the flower of the whole British infantry,
which in their present situation are useless as to the

general operations of the war. The French have more troops in the West India islands, than are necessary for a mere defensive plan. Their magazines are well furnished; the British on their parts are weak in both these respects in that quarter, and I am convinced that the slightest demonstration there, would occasion the immediate removal of General Clinton's army. Some think that the British will keep possession of N. York and Rhode Island, to enable them to make better terms.

There is field for conjecture; the British may at this moment be attempting a negotiation with France. It can be neither her interest nor inclination to sacrifice her ally; a general peace in this case would be the consequence. But accident or the caprice of a minister may disappoint the most rational predictions, and give rise to events which, at present, appear the most improbable.

An unlucky affray has happened at Boston which gives us the deepest concern. We are not acquainted with particulars any farther than that a quarrel arose between some American and French sailors. They proceeded from harsh words to more dangerous blows. Two valuable French officers who attempted to quell the riot were much abused, and one of them, the Count de St Sauveur it is feared will not recover.

Genl Greene informs us that the matter has been generally traced and found to originate with the Convention troops. The sailors who were the immediate instruments were Britons in the privateer service. If this is not strictly true, it is a story which policy w^d encourage.

Genl Greene in his first letter on the subject informs us that the French officers seemed satisfied that the mischief had been planned by some artful hand in Burgoyne's army, but he since tells us that there are jealousies on the subject.

I saw very plainly when I was at Boston, that our antient hereditary prejudices were very far from being eradicated.

A sergeant major who deserted from the 2^d batallion of Highlanders gives Genl Scott the following intelligence. That the 1st and 2^d British brigade had received orders to hold themselves in readiness for embarking for the W. Indies; that the transports are lying in readiness to take them on board; he has heard officers say that New York is to be evacuated. Another deserter asserts that four regiments are already embarked, and that the horse transports as well as others are ordered to prepare for sea.

I omitted to mention to you that Lord Howe was on board a frigate during the whole time that Count D'Estaing gave him chace. This is a privilege allowed to admirals for their personal security, and is analagous to a general's placing himself on a safe eminence to view an engagement, but it could only be used in a desperate case, and by a man of Lord Howe's established reputation.

For want of time to arrange my ideas, I have written you a chaos of intelligence, which I fear you will hardly be able to reduce to any kind of order.

You will not, I hope, quit Philadelphia immediately after the first of next month. A few days more must develop the enemy's intentions, and may give me an opportunity of obtaining a furlough, at a time when it will not be dishonourable to take one. The campaign in all probability will terminate very insipidly, by the evacuation of N. York and Rhode Island, and I shall have time enough to rejoin the army for the Canadian expedition if it should take place.

Anticipating the happiness which I shall enjoy in embracing you, I commend myself to your love, and my dear father to God's protection.

JOHN LAURENS.

Gen¹ Scott informs us that a party of the enemy have advanced on this side Kingsbridge. Another party have landed at Paulus Hook and advanced beyond Bergen. From the description, they are strong foraging parties, and design to glean the county previous to taking leave. Our General has given orders to parry any stroke which they may meditate against our posts in the highlands, tho' the possibility of such an enterprise is exceedingly remote, and their dispositions in this case would be void of common sense.

His Excellency Henry Laurens, Esqʳ.,

President of Congress, Philadelphia.

(Private).

HEAD QUARTERS, *7th October*, 1778.

My Dear Father:

The M. de Lafayette will not long have delayed after his arrival to open to you a plan for introducing French troops into Canada. From the manner in which he explained himself to the General, he seemed to intimate a desire that Congress w^d solicit him to bring about this business, as being sensible of its utility to the United States. He did not expect to succeed in any other way than by intrigues, petticoat interest, &ca. He lays down as self-evident that Canada cannot be conquered by American forces alone; that a Frenchman of birth and distinction at the head of four thousand of his countrymen, and speaking in the name of the Grand Monarque is alone capable of producing a revolution in that country. When he asked my opinion privately on the subject, and asked me what I would say if I were a member of Congress to such a proposition, I replied that I did not think Congress could solicit, or even accept it, because there did not appear a sufficient reciprocity in the benefits to be derived from such an expedition. On the one side there would be an immense expense of transporting troops, loss of valuable officers and soldiers, &ca., in fine, all the disadvantages, and on the other, all the gain. That he did well to say the project could only take place by indirect means, for a minister would not in his cool moments deprive his country of so many troops, with no other view than that of killing so many Englishmen, and conquering an extensive province for us; that he was to reflect that France, tho' powerful in men, had an extensive frontier to guard, and in an European war w^d not have to do with England alone.   This was my private opinion to the Marquis; my still more private opinion is, that we sh^d not give France any new pretensions to Canada.   It is a delicate subject to touch on, but I dare say that we agree in our sentiments, and that the Marquis will be thanked for his good intentions, and his offers waived.

Our last intelligence, from deserters belonging to different corps, and who came out at different times, confirms the intended embarkation of ten regiments for the W. Indies.   The 10th 45th and 52^d they say, were drafted to complete these regiments, and the forage and live stock collected in Jersey are destined for their use.

Genl Scott writes that the enemy are very busy in embarking baggage, as may be discovered from an eminence to which his parties go.

You will see the last unavailing effort of the commissioners in their manifesto.

Your most affectionate

JOHN LAURENS.

HEAD QUARTERS, 13*th* *October*, 1778.

My Dear Father:

I should have been glad to have accompanied Mr Custis, Mrs Washington's son, who is so kind as to take charge of this; but I cannot be ready in less than a week or ten days.

The late bad weather drove that detachment of the enemy, that was posted on Valentine's hill, into the city, and they now confine themselves within Kingsbridge. The detachment in Jersey from which there are daily desertions of two or three, have not yet returned; but they have contracted themselves, and seemed to be wholly employed in collecting and carrying off their spoil. Deserters inform us that they have indiscriminately taken every kind of grain, Indian corn, stock and all. One of the vessels burnt by our parties, had stalls fitted up for twelve horses, and ample provision of water for a sea voyage. We have repeated accounts of the sickliness of Byron's crews. The report of their disorder being contagious is without foundation, as well as that of the British fleets having put to sea in quest of the French.

General Greene who arrived in camp yesterday, gives us an account of Captain Barry's having lost his frigate two days after he sailed from Boston. He engaged a British 32 gun frigate and had fought her with his usual bravery, and great prospect of success; his men and officers being sworn not to surrender;

when a 64 gun ship came up and put an end to the contest; but not before he had given two or three such fires as Barry's situation, relatively to the British frigate, allowed. Our brave captain then avoided violating his oath by running his ship on shoar at Seal island, and keeping up a fire from four guns which he brought to bear in his stern, 'till he got out his boats and some baggage. He made his escape with eighty hands; the rest were to shift for themselves by landing. Ten who concealed themselves have escaped since; one, an Englishman, remained on board and extinguished the fire which Barry put to the ship in order to destroy her, by which means she was saved, and the enemy got her off.

If the Marquis de Lafayette goes to Europe, it is probable that he will take a great many of his countrymen with him. It is almost certain that many of them will be very troublesome to Congress for certificates. Duplessis applied to me the other day to obtain him a furlough for Philadelphia, and to give him a certificate of his having behaved well at the battle of Monmouth, that he might go and signify his design to Congress of retiring from service.

I replied that he had no need of an introduction to the President if he had any business with Congress, that he already had a most honourable certificate from them, and that if he wanted a final certificate at going away, the Commander in chief was the proper person to apply to. The commissions which Congress

30

have applied so liberally have destroyed the value of rank which is the ostensible reward of merit, and have done great injustice to many brave and experienced officers who have found themselves on a par with, or but one remove from some of their countrymen who had no pretensions to rank of any kind. The only reparation that can be made, and it is but a feeble one, is to be sparing in the testimonials to be given at their departure, and to make a pointed difference between those which are given to men of real merit, and those which are the effect only of political management.

You will be so good as to excuse my mentioning these matters; they have occasioned great disgust in foreigners conscious of their worth, much uneasiness in our native officers, and have brought rank into disgrace. In a few days I shall have an opportunity of speaking more fully on this subject and many others if you permit, when I have the happiness of embracing you in Philadelphia. I am anxious to receive a letter from you in the meantime, and begin to count the hours which are to precede my setting out.

My dearest friend and father,

Adieu.

JOHN LAURENS.

The purchasing commissioners complain of the scarcity of flour. Some persons high in public office, are accused of the detestable crime of monopolizing.

Is there no means of bringing their villainy to light, and expelling them from all share of the people's confidence.

His Excellency, Henry Laurens, Esq.,

President of Congress, Philadelphia.

(Private).

Fav^d by I. Custis, Esquire.

INDEX.

CPSIA information can be obtained
at www.ICGtesting.com
Printed in the USA
BVHW072052170720
583829BV00004B/655